MENTAL MODELS:

A Collection of Thinking Tools Helping You To Manage Productivity, Thinking In Systems, To Improve Your Day-To-Day Decision-Making, Problem-Solving and Logical Analysis Skills

By: David Drive

Table of Contents

Introduction

Congratulations on choosing *Mental Models: a Collection of Thinking Tools which Helping You to Manage Productivity, Thinking in Systems, to Improve Your Day-To-Day Decision-Making, Problem-Solving and Logical Analysis Skills*.

The following chapters will discuss what you need to know in order to start using mental models for your own needs. There are a lot of different time management tricks and tips that you can try out, and many of them can work well, but if you want to shorten the time it takes to make decisions, ensure that you will make the best decisions, and overall just make your life a bit easier. This guidebook is going to take some time to discuss what mental models are, how these are going to work for your benefit and the different types of mental models that you can use based on what you would like to solve.

To start this guidebook, we are going to take a look at what mental models are all about. This helps us to see what these models are about and some of the benefits that come with them. We can also look at the power that is behind these mental models, and the ten top mental models that can be used with a lot of the other topics that we will discuss in this guidebook.

After we have some of the basics about mental models organized and ready to go, it is time to dive into some of the practical applications for these mental models and how you can use them for a lot of different aspects and personality types as well. You will find that these mental models work well for making decisions, for entrepreneurs and others parts of running a business, for those who are researching and inquisitive, to help you improve your parenting, for critical thinkers and educators, and even for those who are trying to work on their own personal development. With these topics, we are going to explore more about what these mental models are, and see how they can be used in every part of your life.

To finish off this guidebook, we are going to take a look at some of the different case studies about these mental models. These will help us to see the mental models in works, so we are not just working with theory, we can see the exact ay that these mental models can be used!

A lot of time and effort can be wasted thinking things through and making decisions, and often the longer we sit on these thoughts, the more confused we get. Mental models help us to cut through the clutter by providing us with some of the plans that we need to really get things on track. When you are ready to learn more about these mental models and how they work, make sure to check out this guidebook to help you get started.

There are plenty of books on this subject on the market, thanks again for choosing this one! Every effort was made to ensure it is full of as much useful information as possible, please enjoy!

Chapter 1: An Understanding of the Mental Models

One fact of life that we just can't deny is that our brains will be responsible for everything that the body does. This means that anything that affects our brain will then affect all of the other facets of our lives. Yes, the brainpower is going to rely a lot on its software or the mindset that you have, and the hardware, which is going to be the nerves.

We know it is really hard to work with a system that is sophisticated, with lots of good hardware, and then have some bad software on it. This just ends up being a bit energy-wasting blend of silicon and metal in the computer. In order to help put these mental models into the proper perspective, it is important for us to take a look at some of the different elements that are at the core of this idea, and how we are able to use them to our advantage.

First, we need to take a look at what the model means for our "mental model". A model is simply going to be a microcosmic representation of the real object. This object can be either non-physical or physical, it really doesn't matter. It is going to be like a blueprint, a diagram, a mold, or a map and it is going to depict some of the key features of the real object, without having to bear all of the costs that come with this model being around.

Modeling is something that we are going to see in a lot of technological and scientific endeavors. However, this doesn't mean that we have to leave the models confined to only those two fields.

There may be a ton of different options out there that promise to work on getting things done more effectively, and a lot of promises that are going to try and help you to manage your time and more, but some of the best options out there for you to use are going to be these mental models.

You get to choose which one you use, and the more of them that you learn about, the easier it is to grab one out of your toolbox and put it to good work. This opens up a whole new world of what you are able to do, how easy it is to get tasks done, and how you will be able to succeed in any endeavor that you attempt to do. How many of the other options out there are going to be able to provide what these mental models will provide to you as well?

This does not mean that you can't use some of the tools that are out there and available to those who want to enhance the mental models. And if you are working on things like time management and want to use charts or diagrams or the Pomodoro timer to help you, then this is perfectly acceptable as well. But you will find that working with these mental models can be effective, even without all of the other equipment along for the ride.

There are a lot of core reasons why you may want to take a look at modeling and see how it can work for a lot of different technological and scientific adventures. Some of the most common reasons for this include:

1. A model is going to help you to depict a mental concept, and this makes the model concept a lot easier to understand overall compared to the main concept.

2. The model is going to make it easier and cheaper to present the real object to others.

3. A model is going to be a lot cheaper to make and use than the real object. This means that the cost of creatively destroying the model if needed will be low.

4. A model is easier to adapt to the changes in the main concept than the real object.

5. These models are going to be cost-effective methods to avoid some bigger mistakes. Mistakes, faults, and even misconceptions can be easily detected when we look at the model and

appropriate corrections done to it prior to launching the real object.

While it is true that there are some models that we are able to look at in physical form, there are others that do better when we look at them in virtual form. Physical models are going to be for objects that contain some form such as planes, cars, ships, building, territories and the like. Virtual models, on the other hand, is going to be for things that are not physical, such as the thoughts, imagination, senses, and interpretations.

Mental models are going to fall within the virtual nature above because the mind is not really a physical object. Some of the virtual models that you may see that relate to this could be things like strategic military models, culture models, organization models, and more.

What is a Mental Model?

With this understanding with us, it is time to take this a bit further and look closer at what a mental model is all about. A mental model is going to be a blueprint of how you can boost up the cognitive engine's capacity to make decisions that are more strategic and intelligent. A mental model is going to be just a one-dimensional view of reality. This means that if we want to make sure that we have a better view of multi-dimensional reality, you would need to work with more than one of these mental models at a time. When we are working on a real-life situation, we are going to not rely on a single model but will rely on a mental multi-model instead.

This brings up the question of why these mental models are so important. Just like software is able to help direct some of the functional behavior that we see with a computer, a mental model is going to help to direct some of the functional behavior of your brain, and because of that, it directs the rest of your body as well.

Using the analogy of the computer a bit more, you will be able to more easily see and deduce some of the core reasons that makes it imperative to start using these mental models in your own life. Some of the biggest reasons why these mental models are so prevalent and such a great option for you to use in your life includes:

1. They are efficient: A mental model is going to help the brain learn how to run more efficiently, especially when it comes to dealing with some tasks that may be repetitive and routine. This is going to allow the brain to be more creative and to focus on novel inputs instead.

2. Effectiveness: These mental models are going to help limit the errors that we see, and will make sure there is less wasted effort. This is going to make the brain power more effective in delivering the outcome that you are looking for.

3. Economy: This is a term that is all about the efficient and effective utilization of the resources that we have. the brain is going to need a ton of different resources to help it operate. In fact, you will find that the brain is the most resource-intensive organ in the whole body. Because of this, any increment to the effectiveness and efficiency of the brain means that you are going to use your resources more wisely.

4. Certainty: The mental model is going to help you bring about some level of certainty when it comes to common challenges in your life.

Because of this, a mental model is able to coordinate the brain function of several people inside the same team or group. This means that the model is going to bring in a bit of predictability that you need when it is time to handle challenges and more.

5. Productivity: With certainty and economy added to the mix, the productivity that you will see with the brain is going to go higher. In the end, the productivity of not just the individual person, but also the whole team, is going to go up.

The neat thing is that these mental models are going to be able to do a lot of different things for you. They can first step in and enable you to see the world in a more accurate manner, and then you can use this new form of accuracy to predict the future in a much better way than it would have been without them. This model can also help you to form a new mastermind kind of alliance because you will then be able to find some people who can suit your model and then the connections that are built up from this are going to be mutually beneficial. These connections are important because they will sharpen up the mental model that you have, making them more precise. And finally, the mental model is going to help you to generate some breakthrough ideas because they will have a unique angle view of the situation that is at hand.

Another thing that we need to take a look at before we move on with these mental models is the origins of them, or how they got started. we are not able to tell with a great deal of certainty where these models begin with because it is believed they started at the beginning of time. while we are going to be able to create some mental models deliberately from our knowledge, it is possible to have some mental models that are created in a more instinctive manner.

For example, it is possible to have one of these models etched into the genes. It is going to be these that will help an infant learn how to respond to some of the external stimuli in a certain way that we can predict from the moment they are born. For example, all infants know how to respond to heat and light, how to identify their mother, how to suck, and how to cry, even though they had no chance to learn how to do these things. Over time though, the infant is going to develop some of their own mental models so they learn the best way to communicate and interact with their mother.

Because of this, it is believed that these mental models are going to be as old as humankind. We can call some of them primal mental models. But then there are the mental models that we can create for our own needs, the higher or the secondary mental models. These are the ones that we are going to consciously and deliberately generate out of our learning and some of the practice experiences that we have.

Even with this in mind, some of these secondary models are going to be etched into our genes after some time if we use them in the proper manner. This is done to help future generations learn how to cope and adapt with some of the changing environment that is out there. For example, epigenetics is going to be an interesting field of study that can help us to look this over a bit more as well. In this guidebook, while we recognize that all of the mental models can be important we are going to spend our time focusing mostly on the higher or the secondary models, the ones that adults are going to purposely create to help them make things easier.

How Our Minds Work and Why the Models Help

To help us learn a bit more about these mental models, we first need to take a look at how the mind works and then how the models can come in and make a difference. The best first step that we can take to help understand how the mind works is to look at a computer model. A human-like robotic computer is going to be the closest that we can get to seeing how the mind works for now, so let's focus on that.

Using a computer model, there is going to be a part for the hardware, and a part for the software. The robotic computer is going to have what is known as the main body, which will include the torso and the head, as well as some limbs that are a part of the peripheral limbs. The thinking part of this kind of model is going to rest in the head, just like with us. Inside the head, we are going to see that there is a CPU, which is going to act as the brain of the computer. The visible part of this CPU is going to be the hardware and the parts that we are not able to see will be the software.

In the same way, the brain is going to have parts that are the software and then parts that are the hardware. The part that is the software is going to be the mind. We are able to see the mind as a type of container where our mindset will be able to reside. And the mindset is simply going to be a set of a lot of different software programs we use. Just like the software on a computer has several sets of programs that are meant to play their own role, this helps to make sure that everything functions the way that it does.

To clarify, the mind is going to be like the software. And the mindset is going to be the collection of a unique set of instructions, or programs, that will each tell the brain how to execute the specific functions that it should. When it comes to working with computer software, we do have the system software as well as the application software.

To start with the system software, this is going to be the part of the brain that will manage all of the internal functions of our mind, with regards to how it is going to properly manage any resources that it has. The application software is going to comprise of different sets of programs, and each one is going to be designed to execute specific functions when it is triggered by some kind of stimuli that is external, such as the environment. Because of this, the Application software is going to be based on the environment that is around it. This could be more specific by talking about how to interact productively with the external environment.

The software itself, which is going to be our mindsets here, is going to be crafted more like an interface that works between the external environment and the internal environment. This software is going to be crafted based on a lot of different models. First off, the "System software" in the mind is going to be based on some of the internal things that we hold inside the body. Then the "Application software" is going to be crafted based on how the external model outside of the body is behaving.

However, we will see that the actual interface that happens between the two of these needs to be both external and internal features. They have to be able to work well together in order to get the mind to work the way that we want. The external model is going to be more dynamic compared to the internal one. The reason for this is because the external environment is going to be more dynamic and fluid, and this results in us needing more dynamism, adaptability, and flexibility in our application model.

This means that we need to make sure that the Application model is going to turn out multidimensional as if in a way to obey Adam Smith's concept of the many-sided man. This is the reason why we are going to have hundreds, if not more of these Application models, which are going to come about naturally because humans have a big desire to cope with the external environment that is always changing around them.

It is going to be on the basis of this multidimensional and many-sided perspective that this book is able to establish some of the foundations that we are going to work on. Our goal is to explore, dissect, and then synthesize some of the best mental models that are established, ones that have been put together to make it easier for humans to cope with the ever-changing environment that is all around them.

It is common for a lot of us to feel lost in the modern world, trying to adapt to things that are always changing and we may not always know how to deal with these kinds of situations. But with the help of these mental models, we can better understand the world around us, become more adaptable, make better decisions, and so much more.

Mental models are going to be one of the best things that you can work on for your best health, for your creativity, and for your own efficiency. They may sound a bit more confusing right now, but as we go through this guidebook and you see a few of the examples of how they can work, it will make more sense what we are doing here, and why you would benefit so much from using some of these mental models.

The Benefits of These Mental Models

There are a number of benefits that come with using mental models. This is why so many people enjoy using them to help make decisions easier, to help them with time management, and to make things easier overall. If you are someone who struggles to manage their time or to make some of the important decisions you need and even end up making the wrong decision in a lost of situations, then it is time to use these mental models.

The first benefit that comes with these mental models is that there are so many of them to learn about. There are believed to be hundreds of these mental models that you are able to choose from. While most of these are going to be variations on some of the most common mental models, you will find that you still get a lot of different choices when it comes to the kind of mental model that you need to use in different situations. You are not stuck with one or two models that you have to work with, and if you don't want to use one, and you don't like it, you don't get any options. Mental models come in a variety of types and choices, so you can find the one that works the best for you.

You will like that they can be customizable for your needs. You can take any of the mental models that we have in this guidebook, and customize them for your needs. We will take a look at a few examples of how you are able to change this around a bit, and use the same mental model in different manners along the way. This helps you to find the right mental model,

These mental models can work for almost any kind of situation that you need in life. We are going to take some time to look at many of the situations where you are able to use these mental models and the different types of mental models that you are able to use in the process. This will help us to see that no matter what kind of situation we encounter in our lives, we can rely on these mental models to help us out.

These mental models can make decision making easier. There are a lot of different types of mental models that you can choose from, and many of them can help you to really take control of the decisions you make. indecision is going to really cause us to fall behind and miss out on some of the best opportunities out there. We also worry that we are going to make the wrong decisions along the way, which can make it harder for us to know when we should slowdown and when we can speed up when it comes to making decisions for every aspect of life.

Mental models are able to come into the scene and solve this kind of problem. They are set up so that you can eliminate the bad choices right away, or even learn how to go with one of the first options that you think about because these are often the best, and then just jump right in. We waste too much time with indecision and we make the wrong decisions because we just have too many options to choose from. With these mental models, we learn the right steps to take to get things done, and often this helps us to make better decisions than we did before.

Time management can become a breeze when you start to use these mental models for your needs. Do you struggle with being able to manage the time that you have in a day? Do you feel like you are working hard to do all of your work, but you get to the end of the day, and you are so far behind that you have no idea how you will get it all done?

Many people are going to struggle when it comes to time management. They feel like they are doing a lot of work, but then they are always behind and won't be able to get it done on time. Often it is more about taking care of the right tasks at the right time, minimizing the things that distract you, and getting your mind to stay on track.

The right mental model is going to make this happen. We will talk about a lot of different types of mental models that can work to make you more efficient, to help you get more of your work done quickly and to keep you on track. Utilizing these don't only make your work easier, you may find that you can get the work done, with a little extra time, helping you to leave work with nothing left undone, and less stress overall.

Mental models can be a great addition to your life because they can really change up your view of the world. And often this is in a positive manner. Too many times we spend our efforts concentrating on things that take too much time, debating against too many decisions, and even dealing with procrastination. These mental models are going to come into play because they help us to take control over these problem areas, and focus our attention on how to get things done, and get them done in a quick and efficient manner.

And with all of the different options that you are able to work with when it comes to these mental models, you are sure to find the one that works the best for you, no matter what kind of situation you are dealing with. Think about how much easier your life can be, and how much more you can get done on a regular basis when you are able to implement these mental models in an effective manner.

Mental Models Affect the Way that You Are Going to View the World Around You

It is important to remember that these mental models are going to be a unique way to look at the world. They are going to be a set of tools that you are able to use to help you think in a more effective manner. Each mental model is set up in a manner that is different, with a framework that helps you to look at life, or even at an individual problem that is coming your way.

While there are a lot of ways that you are able to work with mental models, you will find that they really shine when you use them to develop more than one manner to look at the same problem. For examples, let's say that you would like to make sure that you avoid procrastination and make sure that your day is more productive.

If you understand some of the different mental models that we will talk about in this guidebook, then you are going to have a range of options that you can use to determine your priorities, and actually get things done.

Remember here that one mental model is not necessarily any better than one of the others. It just depends on which one you like the most, and which one seems to be the best for you. These mental models are going to work to give you a large range of options that will help you determine your priorities while getting important things done in the process. When you have a lot of different mental models available to use, it is easier to pick out the one that is going to work the best for your current situation, rather than only using the one that you have learned how to use.

The Law of the Instrument

According to Abraham Kaplan in "The Conduct of Inquiry", the Law of the Instrument is going to be important. This one is going to be based on the idea that if you give a hammer to a small boy, then the boy is going to find that everything he encounters needs pounding. We can look at this in a similar manner as if you only have one framework for thinking about the world, then you are going to try to take each problem that comes to you into that framework, and that doesn't always work. But if you have a set of mental models to work with, your potential for finding a solution is going to increase.

One thing that is also interesting with this one is that the problem you are facing is going to become more pronounced as your expertise in an area starts to grow. If you are talented in one area, you re going to have a tendency to believe that your skillset is going to be the answer to most of the different problems that you face. The more that you start to master a single mental model, then the more likely it is that this will be your downfall, simply because you will rely on it too much.

This is why we need to work to have a bigger toolbox of mental models, you are going to improve your ability to solve a lot of problems. This is because you provide yourself with more options for getting the answer that is right. When your toolbox is full of lots of different mental models, you will be better set up to choose the best tool for the given situation.

Chapter 2: The Power of Mental Models

Now that we have had a bit of time to look at these mental models and get a feel for what they are all about, it is time to stop and look at some of the roles, and the powers, that these mental models are going to be able to do this. To help us to get a better understanding of this topic though, we need to first break down the mental model into its core characteristics and elements.

A mental model, when it is done in the right manner, is going to comprise itself of an indistinguishable mix of interpretations and facts. With that in mind, there are four core elements that come with this kind of model, and those four components are going to include:

1. It interprets: A good mental model is going to act as a type of context that can grant meaning to the given observation. This kind of observation can include things like relationships, people, circumstances and events. While granting some room for context, the mental model is going to give them more of an appearance of objective reality.

2. It disguises: As this model is going to grant some kind of observation an appearance of objective reality, it is also able to help disguise our interpretations of this observation as the only Truthful reality. This interpretation is going to be achieved in a variety of manners including collective agreements, position statements, deliberations, and explanations.

3. It determines: After being able to disguise our interpretations as an objective reality, it is going to exclude all of the other possibilities

because it deems these as unreasonable, impossible, or illogical. Because of this, it is going to fence off this interpretation and will block out all of the alternative interpretations that can come in.

4. It dictates. This mental model is going to eventually start to dictate some of the beliefs that we have about certain topics, our actions, our behaviors, our habits, and our attitudes in such a manner that it helps to make the interpretation we have to appear more of objective reality.

In addition to the four core principles that we just listed above, you will find that there is going to be a fundamental attribute that goes along with this idea, and that is going to be the idea of invisibility. Being invisible simply means that the fallacies of interpretation become hard to detect or notice by those who hold the interpretation as truthful reality.

While facts remain facts no matter what your interpretation is, interpretations are going to be as good as the mind of the one holding onto them. Because of this, the interpretations can't be taken without the beholder's opinions, reasons, judgments, biases, and presumptions being a big part of how they see that situation.

This brings up the question of how many of these mental models actually exist? We know that there are a lot of different methods that you can use in order to come up with your interpretation of things and to see the world in a certain way. But we need to take it a bit further and explore more of what we are able to do with these mental models and why they are so different. The four primary types of mental models that you are able to work with, and that we will concentrate on in this guidebook, include:

1. The individual mental model
2. The identity mental model
3. The collective mental model
4. The fundamental mental model.

Each one of these mental model types is going to play a different role in how we are able to perceive the world, how we can actually create our own unique perception of reality, and how we can even start and enter into some of the relationships that we have with those around us. Let's dive into this a bit more and explore some of the different types of mental models and how they each work.

The Fundamental Mental Model or FMM

The first model that we are going to take a look at is the Fundamental Mental Model. The primary power and role that comes with the FMM is that they are going to determine how we think and what we can or can't think about, what is possible, and what is not possible. We will find in our study of FMM that there are two primary types to focus on and these will include:

1. The FMM is going to advocate for OR and EITHER. But not for AND and WITH. The keyword for this model is going to be OR.
2. The FMM that is able to advocate for AND and WITH, but not for EITHER and OR. The keyword that is used with this one will be AND.

The FMM OR model is only going to be able to switch between two possibilities so that is all that you can work with. For example, me OR you would show us how this model works. Whenever this FMM OR is showing up, it is going to have the power to create exclusivity, separations, and some divisions, so be ready to see some conflict show up with this one over some of the others. It is going to be pretty egocentric with power as well.

It is going to be the OR mental model that will show us more about individualism and will allow the individual to be above the nation, above society, and any other grouping form. It is going to place the personal individual identity above the crowd and it doesn't like to share the limelight. You will find that with this one, you become an abominable presupposition, especially when it comes to things like ownership, possession, privileges, and rights.

The OR model is going to create a type of world view where things are always black and white, with no areas of grey to go along with it. There is true or false, right or wrong, and good or bad in this kind of world. While the OR model is going to be good in that it advances the individual, personal effort, and lots of creativity, it can also be negative because it could include things like loneliness and greed in the process.

The World of OR

Collective MM is not necessarily devoid of the FMM OR. When a group of individuals coalesces against another group, these are going to be collective actions that still have individualism, identity ego, and some of the other attributes that we could see with the FMM OR. Collective MM in the world of OR can be seen as those in collective OR entities, including regional, national, and religious, along with anything else that would promote a configuration that is US vs. THEM.

When economics claim the power of money, politics are going to claim the power of the law, science will step in to claim the power of knowledge, and religion will finish it out with some claims to the power of truth. When these groups do actions like this, they are doing manifestations of the Collective MM within the world of FMM OR.

This does not mean that a collective MM is only going to exist hand in hand with the FMM OR. It just means that you can find some of the collective MM inside of this mental model as well. Not all collectives are going to see the world in the view of us vs. them, but some of them will.

As we have seen, lots of different groups can be a Collective MM within the FMM OR world. These entities are going to attain a unique identity that will help them to stand out from the rest of the world. For example, one religious entity could claim to be the one that holds onto the absolute truth while claiming that some of the other religious entities are only spreading falsehoods. As such, this kind of religious entity is going to be able to identify itself back to God, while claiming that the other religious entities around can only have 'gods' instead.

Nationalities are often going to claim exclusive ownership of a given territory, and then they would issue National Identity Cards just to those whom the political system within that nationality is going to identify as citizens. Those who are seen as the non-citizens are not going to get the National IDs and they will have to get things like a passport or a visa before they can temporarily reside, pass through, or even enter that identified territory.

We can seven see this happen when we work with a political system. You may have one kind of political system that claims to be the only one that has any civility, while it brands the other competitor as backward, barbaric, or primitive. As such, it is able to pass laws that will grant itself the power to do what it would like to rule over, settle, and invade while grabbing from nations that it claims are from the backward system. This is stuff that has been seen with neo-colonialism, colonialism, and slavery.

You can also think of the so-called democratic world employing tools like genocide, military force, and assassination in order to bring things like liberty and freedom to other countries. Think of the "communist world" that was trying to heal up the failures that it says is in the democratic world through revolutions that usher in collectivity and equality, which then ended up with some of the most brutal dictators and genocides in our history.

These are just a few of the examples of what can happen with the collective mental model. It can definitely be more than one person who steps in and takes control like this to get what they want. They may have a good message attached to it, but the basics that it comes down to will be the idea of US vs. THEM and that we are better than others.

In the name of Identity MM, millions of people have ended up losing their lives, millions in Europe during the world wars, millions in the Soviet Union during the Bolshevik Revolution, and so on. The world of OR, whether it comes from individual MM, identity MM, or collective MM has the power to breed a lot of brutality, wars, and conflict if it is not used in the proper manner.

This, of course, doesn't mean that the FMM OR is going to be bad or dangerous all of the time. it is going to be based on the person and on the truthful reality that they decide to focus on. Individual power is not always a bad thing, and if it is used in the proper manner, it can be a really good thing too. There are a lot of benefits that we are able to see with this individual power. For example, individual power is going to enable someone to:

1. Be right and fight off any wrongs.
2. Avoid having other people control us all of the time.
3. Avoid looking bad, by learning how to look good
4. How to avoid being dominated while dominating ourselves.

The important thing to remember when we are working with the FMM OR mental model is that the world is not going to be just black or white. The extreme of any of the above mentioned can, of course, be dangerous, this is why this kind of mental model needs to be measured out. This is why we need to bring in some of the other mental models in order to ensure that there is always a healthy balance present to work with.

The World of AND

Now that we have had a chance to talk about the world of OR, and what can happen when that individuality and that it can become a bad thing when it is taken too far, whether by the individual or by a group, it is time to switch gears for a moment and look a bit at the world of AND>

As you can imagine, learning how to shift away from the FMM OR can be a good thing. This is because some of the hallmarks that end up with the FMM AND are going to include things like mutually beneficial collaborations, peaceful unity, and genuine partnerships. It is only from this kind of context that the collective MM is going to craft a powerful and sustainable team spirit.

This does not mean that you have to give up your individuality. But it does mean that you see that the world is not about you vs. them. Both parties can benefit, and live in more peace and harmony when we view the world through the lens of the FMM AND.

With this kind of worldview, we are going to see that the world can provide us with a WIN-WIN outcome in each scenario. This doesn't mean that there won't be times when it is difficult and when things are not going to always work out the way that we would like. But it does ensure that we keep an open mind during the process of communication and that both parties will be open to hearing the other side, making some compromises, and coming up with solutions that are the best for both.

It is only in this kind of world where we are going to see that the ceiling for development will be removed and that the sky is no longer a big limit for us to reach with others. Instead, the sky becomes one of our milestones along the way. true education is what will open up all of the different possibilities so that we end up with a world of more FMM AND.

Now, there are benefits that work with the OR and the AND world view. The best mental models that are out there will be able to hide the negatives while balancing out the benefits that come with FMM AND along with the FMM OR. It is a mental model that is able to optimize the benefits that come with both worlds, the idea of collectivism and individualism.

This is not always going to be easy. When you do this, you will pretty much be working on a nice balancing act that can hardly stay perfect all of the time, thanks to our ever-changing world. As such, it is going to be a journey, not a final destination point, that is going to include a lot of improvement, change, discovery, and exploration along the way.

Creating the best mental model for you and for those around you can be tough. You want to make sure that you are taking care of yourself and not getting others to walk all over you. And there is certainly nothing wrong with having an individual spirit and wanting to stand strong against others at times. But we can see what can happen when the OR MM goes too far.

We need to be able to combine both the OR and the AND model together in order to allow us to get some of what we want in the process, while also taking care of the other person in the mix, and not causing them a lot of harm in the process. And while this may seem like such a monumental task right now, we are going to take an even closer look at the different mental models, and how you can do exactly that, as we go through this guidebook.

Chapter 3: Some of the Most Common Mental Models

The neat thing about these mental models is that there are actually quite a few of them that you are able to work with. This allows you to think and act in many different manners and can help you when it is time to make some big decisions. With this in mind, we are going to focus on the top ten mental models, even though there are at least 80 of these models that can be applicable to our modern world. The top ten mental models that we are going to focus on in this chapter will include:

The Map is Not the Territory

The rationale that we are going to follow with this model is that the way we are able to see the world isn't really itself. Rather, the worldview that we have is going to be based on our own mental construct. A map is just going to be the mental construct that we use. Territorial borders are going to change over time, and things around us can change as well.

In a greater perspective, the map is not the territory will warn us against some of the logical fallacy that occurs when we confuse the labels, semantics, and artifacts with the things that are real. Some of the other fallacies that are similar to this will include misplaced concreteness and reification. Each one of us is going to have or own mental map that helps us to view the world. Yet the world is really complex, and it is impossible for a human to totally comprehend what is going on. This means that our attitudes, beliefs, assumptions, and conclusions are not going to be the best parameters all of the time for helping us to understand the totality of the real world.

When it is time to look at our communication and interpersonal relationships, it is likely that we are going to try and impose our own mental map onto others, or we think that they should be able to read our mental map. But we have to remember that the other people we are around have their own mental maps as well, and they would like us to follow theirs instead of ours. This is where a lot of misunderstanding, confusion, and sometimes extreme conflict, is going to come into the picture.

Yes, it is possible for two people to be in the same place, and even see the same situation or circumstance, but then leave with a different experience. With these different experiences, we are going to see that there are different interpretations and different worldviews in the process. If this is the mental model that you are going with, remember that you should not try to impose your worldview on others, just try to make yourself understood, while also accepting the worldviews of others.

There are several ways that you are able to apply these mental models in your life. These include:

1. Decision making
2. Relationship management

3. Leadership

The Circle of Competence

There is no one who has all of the knowledge in the world. There are always going to be some blind spots in our competencies and the knowledge that we have. it is important that we acknowledge the things that we don't know. This is not a bad thing to not know everything, because it is just not possible. Focusing on the things that we do know, and seeing how that can move us ahead in life is so much better.

Through the circle of competencies, you are going to be able to open up your mind to some more learning. You will be able to avoid some of the common assumptions and fallacies along the way. You can work to discard the ignorant ego and become more reasonable in your understanding the extent of the competency that you have.

This is going to benefit you so much. It can help you to know where your strengths are, and your weaknesses. It is able to point you in the direction that you need to break away from the cocoon of mediocrity and will help you to connect with the right kinds of people so that you are able to learn more from them and grow your knowledge base. Some of the different applications that you can use with the circle of competence will include:

1. Career development and advancement
2. Decision making

First Principles Thinking

It is going to be a lot more about separating the underlying facts and the ideas from the assumptions that you are able to make. when you decide to apply the first principle of thinking, you will be able to decompose a problem into its constituent elements, or to the root causes that are present, and then it is easier to deal with them in the most appropriate manner, rather than running around and hoping that you make the right decisions along the way.

You are able to isolate out some of the pathogens that will cause you the disease from its symptoms. And because of this, you will end up providing some healing to the disease, rather than just some relief to the symptoms that you are feeling. Reaching to the depth of the constituent elements, you will find that you can use these elements to build up to something that is brand new. Some of the applications that you are going to see with this one include:

1. Decision making
2. Problem-solving
3. Engineering
4. Chemistry
5. Medicine

The Pursuit of Knowledge That is Liquid

Solid knowledge is going to be comprised of pellets that are going to be collected into silos. For example, you could have biology silo, a physics, silo, mathematical silos and so on and solid knowledge is hardly going to be fluid, hardly dynamic at all, and hardly flows.

Great free thinkers are going to go beyond the solid knowledge that is offered in schools to the liquid knowledge that is uncondensed, unrefined, and freely flowing. This kind of thinking is going to be a knowledge gathered from your own experiences, from your own discoveries, and your own exploration. This allows you to have a nice adventure while you work on your discovery of knowledge, which can make things easier and more pleasurable along the way.

Thought Experiment

Thought experiments are going to be devices of the imagination that are then used in order to investigate the nature of the things around us. Thought experiments are going to be essential any time that you would like to break into new frontiers, especially when you are trying to go into new and unknown territory. This territory can be unknown and new to you, or they can be unknown to others as well. This kind of thought experiment is going to allow one to crack the impossible, evaluate the potential consequences, and then compare these consequences with some of the known to help them make some informed deductions.

You will find that, in a manner different than some of the empirical examinations that you can do, thought experiment is going to be conducted just in the mind, even though you are able to demonstrate it physically in order to prove it. As such, this kind of mental model is going to be known as a laboratory of the mind instead.

Galileo is actually one of the famous scientists who worked with this thought experiment to help come up with some of the scientific principles that are still seen to be true today. Albert Einstein also used this method as well. The biggest challenge that comes with this kind of mental model is that, without being able to prove it empirically, it is something that we are not able to prove as true or false. Thus, there are some philosophers who are going to consider it more of a mental modeling of the physical realm instead. Some of the applications of this mental model will include:

1. It can help you to research the formulation of your hypothesis.
2. Scenario simulation and synthesis.
3. Scientific exploration

Second-Order Thinking

The first question that we may have here is whether or not there is a First Order? Of course, there is! Before we start to take a look at this Second Order of thinking, we need to do a brief introduction to what the First Order is all about and then compare the two.

When we are working with the First Order thinking, people are going to make decisions that are hasty and quick, ones that are based on what they can see on the surface and in appearances. Because of this quick decision making, the person is not going to be able to go into the depth that they should to understand why things turn out the way that they are. They react quickly, on first impressions, without actually focusing on what is happening and whether they should react in this manner or not.

Then we have the Second Order thinking. With this one, the person is going to take their thinking and decision-maker a bit further. They are going to study some more of the fundamentals that are behind the phenomenon so that they can identify the various variables that are behind this as well.

Those who end up using the Second order thinking, rather than rushing into the decision and going into the decision too quickly, may find that they make a decision that contradicts what their First Order thinking would have done. Let's take a look at an example of how to do this. When there is an explosion that happens, the First Order thinkers are going to try to run away because they assume that the explosion was from a bomb and they want to get away from the danger as quickly as possible.

But then there are the Second Order thinkers. Even though they may want to follow their instincts and take flight, they will be more likely to pause and think about what it could be that caused the explosion, figure out if they are close to the explosion, and then figure out what they could do about it. Maybe they find out that it was just a big tire that burst by them and there was no reason to run off and be scared of it.

So, in some manners of thinking, the First Order thinkers are going to reach to the already existing mental image that is in the mind of this kind of thinker. The actual occurrence that shows up is going to just be the trigger for that action, but not the cause of the action.

Another good example of First Order to Second Order thinking is in the sphere of investment. For example, if Company A declares that there is a profit warning, most First Order thinkers are going to anticipate that the price of the share is about to fall. Because of this, they are going to rush to get rid of the shares as quickly as possible. This causes the shares to happen, but this is because the traders jump in too quickly, not because the value of the shares actually went down.

On the other hand, we can see that a Second Order thinker is going to have done the process of a fundamental analysis on the profit warning to figure out what is going to cause that profit warning. This could easily be something small, like a new investment decision that resulted in less profit, but a bigger asset base. This means that if you hold onto the shares, there may be a temporary dip thanks to the First Order thinkers, but overall, your value from the shares are going to heat back up.

There are a lot of different times when you will be able to use the idea of First Order vs. Second Order mental model to help you make decisions. Some of the best applications of this mental model are going to include:

1. Decision making of any kind
2. In a fundamental analysis
3. Investment decisions
4. Emergency response

Occam's Razor

This is a model that is going to posit that the simple explanations are the ones that are more likely to be true, rather than going for the explanations that are more complex. So, if you are using this mental model, you will find that it works the best if you can pick out a solution that has fewer assumptions in it.

What this means is that when someone makes a decision, they need to be able to minimize the assumptions as much as possible, with the help of experimentation, study, and research before they implement a new decision concept that they want. In case there is not a lot of leeway in the amount of time that is available, then the concept that has the fewest assumptions is the one that is considered the most ideal for implementing.

The reason for this is that when you have more assumptions present, the risk of having some decision errors is going to be higher. Some of the applications of this mental model is going to include:

1. Personal development
2. Career choices

3. Management

4. Leadership

5. Decision making

Inversion

The next mental model that we are going to take a look at is inversion. Inversion is the idea that you will think backward. With this one, you are going to create some likely scenarios after the action or decisions and then you need to seek out how to address all of the scenarios before you decide on which course to take, or before you decide to execute it. This means that you need to be able to approach the problem from the opposite of the natural starting point.

Let's take a look at an example of this. You may be considering a separation or a divorce from your spouse. Before you jump into this and go ahead with some of the divorce proceedings, by inversion, you would stimulate some of the potential scenarios that would happen with this. It could include a strained relationship with your in-laws, loss of your home, increased costs of childcare, loss of your partner, property division and more. If possible, you can then start to mitigate some of the adverse effects of these scenarios before deciding for or against the divorce.

To make this one work a bit better, you have to make sure that you attack your decisions by going backward. This helps you to really plan things out, imagine that things are already done, and consider what decision is actually going to give you the results that you are looking for.

Some of the different applications for the inversion mental model will include the following:

1. Career choice
2. Leadership
3. Decision making
4. Personal development
5. Family planning

Probabilistic Thinking

When you work with probabilistic thinking, you are going to use a variety of probability tools, including statistical tools, to help them approximate the likelihood that a certain event is going to occur. There are two major technologies that already use this including machine learning and artificial intelligence. Some of the different applications of using probabilistic thinking as a mental model will include:

1. Strategic planning
2. Actuarial science
3. Computer sciences, especially when we look at machine learning and artificial intelligence
4. Decision making
5. Investment

Hanlon's Razor

The best look at what the Hanlon mental model is all about is "never attribute malice to that which can be simply explained by stupidity". The gist of this is that you should never assume that something bad is happening because of the wicked intents of others on the situation. Sometimes it is just incompetence or stupidity on the part of the actor, rather than some malice on their part. Stupidity, in this case, can be from the other person, or from you. It is possible that your own stupidity is causing problems because you made the wrong assumption, but then it could be the stupidity of the other person as well.

Due to the egocentric view that most of us have of things, which, in our subconscious minds, assumes that everything in the world revolves around us, we end up assuming a prominent role in the story of everyone else, even though this isn't true. This means that when we are around someone who seems a bit annoyed, we assume that it has to do with us and that we have made them made. When another person is rude to us, it is because they are angry at us or just being mean to us. When we see that someone doesn't want to congratulate us, we assume that they are feeling jealous of us.

As part of the stupidity that comes with us, we are going to perceive some negative responses as malice against us, without being able to consider that it is often due to factors that have nothing to do with us. Hanlon's Razor model is going to be helpful because it can avoid paranoia, anxiety, and stress. It will eventually save us from taking a bad situation and making it worse.

When we use this mental model, we have to understand that to be human is to err, and that there are times when people make mistakes, and even we are going to make some mistakes on occasion. This means that we need to find out if there are other explanations for what has occurred, rather than assuming that there is some malice that comes with this. This is why with Hanlon's razor, it is always best to assume the best intentions or some good faith before we try to prove otherwise.

Some of the applications that we are going to see with the Hanlon's razor will include:

1. Relationship management
2. Decision making
3. Diplomacy
4. Conflict resolution
5. Crisis management

As you can see, there are a lot of different mental models out there that will help you to make decisions, based on the way that you see the world and the point of view that you are looking for along the way as well. Each of these can be effective and ill help you to see some of the results that you want with making decisions that are going to be based on sound judgment, rather than on our emotions or something else that can be subjective. You can determine which of these mental models, as well as some of the others we will talk about in this guidebook that you would like to use to help you make some good decisions and to ensure you can make the best decisions for yourself.

Chapter 4: The Right Mental Model for Those Who Like to Make Decisions

In one case or another, everyone is going to have to make some decisions at one point or another. We all will have to make some decisions. However, there are going to be those who have to make a lot of decisions, and they are often leaders in some key organization. In this chapter, we are going to take a look in particular at some of the best mental models that can be used for those who have to make decisions on a regular basis that impact a company, and those who just need some help making some decisions.

Circle of Influence

The first mental model that we are going to take a look at here is going to be the circle of influence. Before you are able to make a decision, you need to understand where you excel and what your skills are in terms of expertise and knowledge. Then you need to also know some of your weaknesses when it comes to expertise, skills, and knowledge. This is going to give you a nice springboard to work from so you know where to go, what options are not the best and more. This ensures that you are able to keep your decisions towards areas where you excel while staying away from ones where you don't. from there, it is easier for you to slowly expand out the areas of competence in terms of depth and spread when it is time.

The neat thing here is that there are a few different mental models that you are able to use that fit in with this kind of idea. Some of the most common options are going to include:

1. Availability heuristics

This one is going to be based on the idea of "if something can be recalled, then it is important. If it can't be recalled, then it is not important". We can also think of this one like out of sight, out of mind. When we are on this kind of model, the things that come to our mind right away will provide us with the best solutions to the challenges that we are dealing with.

This means that you should not have to struggle as much to find the solutions that you need to the challenges that you have. you should be able to find the solution based off some of the first ones that come to your mind. You should also choose to use the tools and the concepts that you have mastered, and some of the practical methods that you are competent in, to help you out with this. This helps to keep things simple and doesn't waste time on learning new skills right away (you can learn them as you go), and on looking for an idea when you are going to pick one of the first you came up with anyway.

2. Regret minimization framework

When we are working with this kind of model, you will first need to look at your present away from some moment in the future. You can move into the future and think about how you would feel concerning that situation or that decision later on. Think in terms of "how I feel that I did this, and it happened and succeeded". If you feel that the result of doing an action will lead you to the least amount of regret in the process, then this is the one that you are going to choose to go with.

Inversion

We talked about this one a bit before, but we are going to explore how you can use this to help you make some of the decisions that you need in life. Inversion is a mental model that is all about thinking backward. When you are doing inversion, you are going to create out a few scenarios after your action and your decision, and then seek out ways that you are able to address each scenario that you pick before going with the decision or executing it.

Let's pretend that we are working as a startup entrepreneur. In this role, you may have the right ambition that requires you not only to use your savings and other available funds but also to borrow some more to get it done. Some of the questions that you may be asking yourself about this kind of decision is what if I go bankrupt? What if the idea is a bad one and fails? What if I succeed beyond even my expectations?

From these questions, you would then be able to use the strategy of inversion to help you deal with each in their turn on the plan. You are going to be much better off with this than someone who is only driven by some of their blind ambitions and ho have not put into place some fail-safe options. Inversion is not meant to make you pessimistic about life, but it is more about having some assured optimism that can then be guarded by prudence. From the foregoing to visible benefits, you can see that inversion works because:

1. It is going to be the most helpful when it comes to deconstructing a problem than using the traditional forward-thinking.

2. It is going to help you to weigh the consequences of your decision or your action before you try to execute them. This helps you to stay grounded, calm, and more assured of yourself in the process.

3. It is going to safeguard your enterprise from the vagaries of primitive, raw, and unbridled ambitions.

The Contrarian Approach to Motivation

The next option of mental models that can help out a lot when you are working with making important decisions is known as the contrarian approach to motivation. Motivation is often going to have some raw emotions, unchecked ambitions, and self-ego attached to them. To someone who is a strategic thinker, the worst blunder is to be taken over by these three things. Stripping yourself of the motivation when you are thinking critically is going to help you to really make the best decision, without falling into the trap of thinking with your emotions instead of your head.

The Why Model

Every action or decision that you want to work with is going to have a 'why' attached to it, whether it is implicit or explicit, known or unknown ahead of time. because of this, whenever a certain thing does happen, the most imperative question that anyone needs to ask here, especially when they are the leader, is Why?

Why is what is going to breed the mission. A mission in this sense is going to be the grandest why. This is the main core of every venture or every endeavor that you decide to work on, whether it is in your business or otherwise. When you see a mission lacking, then you will notice that the direction is lacking as well. In the profound noise of confusion, there is always going to be a silent cry of Why that needs to be answered.

Unfortunately, not until someone, usually a leader, listens to this kind of cry, and then answers it, the noise is going to persist. This is a noise that is often heard in wars, crises, conflicts and more.

This one is going to ask us to look at the root cause of why things are happening when they do, the way they do, and more. When we learn the why of something, we are better able to find the right solution that is going to help us take care of the issue, and get it to work the way that we want. This is one of the best ways for you to work with making some of your decisions because it helps you to cut out some of that noise.

The Eisenhower Matrix

When we look at the principle of the Eisenhower matrix, it is simply going to state that what is important is rarely urgent, and what is urgent is rarely important. Of course, there is going to be some grey area that falls between the circle of what is important and the circle of what is the most urgent because it is possible that something is going t0 be urgent and important. This is the thing that you will have to get done and make your foremost priority. Nonetheless, according to this kind of matrix, it is going to be important to take all of your tasks and categorize them into four different groups including:

1. Urgent and important
2. Important, but not really seen as urgent.
3. Urgent but not that important
4. Neither important nor urgent

All of our tasks are going to fall within these four categories. Implementation priority needs to be ranked in the same order. If something falls into the last category, then it is best if you are able to just discard it. Most of the tasks that fall into groups three and two need to be delegated if possible, the ones that you need to do in group two have to be scheduled for a later performance, and then the tasks that fall into the first group are the ones that you need to focus on doing right away.

The Pareto Principle

The Pareto principle is going to be the idea of 80:20. This is a principle that states that 80 percent of our outcomes are going to be generated by 20 percent of our efforts. This means that if we are trying to improve our levels of productivity, then we need to identify the 20 percent of these efforts, and then put the majority of our focus on that. We also have to realize that it is worth it to sacrifice some of the 80 percent of our efforts in order to do this because all that work is only yielding the 20 percent.

The Pareto principle is going to be all about focusing our energies on what is going to matter the most. If something falls inside the least productive spheres, then it is time to discard it. If it still happens to be worth pursuing, it is the best candidate for you to delegate or outsource to someone else to get it done if you don't have the time.

The Paradox of Choice

The last mental model that we are going to take a look at is the paradox of choice. This one is going to hold to the idea that the more choices there are to go from, the more confusing it can be to make a decision at all. And this often results in us making the wrong decision because of this confusion and all of the choices that come with it.

We often think that it is better to have a lot of choices. This gives us some freedom in the process and can make it easier for us to get the results that we want. But in most cases, this is just going to make the situation much worse, and it is not going to help us to make any good decisions at all.

To help us avoid the paradox of choice, we need to learn how to narrow down our choices as much as possible. If we have twenty options to choose from, we need a system that quickly gets us down to five r fewer. The fewer that we are able to get ourselves down too, the easier it is to make not only a good decision but the right decision for us.

Making decisions is something that can take a lot of time. We miss out on a lot of opportunities and feel a lot of stress and anxiety about working with making decisions because we don't know the method that we should pick out or which one is going to be the best for us. The mental models that we discussed in this chapter are meant to show you some really quick methods that you can use to get those decisions made so you can pick the right one for you and move on with the rest of your day.

Chapter 5: Mental Models to Help You Become the Best Entrepreneur

The next type of mental model that we are going to take a look at are ones that work the best for business practitioners and entrepreneurs. The business field can be really wide, and this allows for a wide array of mental models to apply to this. We are going to focus mainly on some of the fields for you to use within the business fields to make this work a bit easier. Let's get started!

Mental Models for Marketers

Marketing is a very crucial function for any business to be successful. Marketers are going to play the role of getting the information about a company out to the public so that they can make good decisions about what to purchase and from whom. But which of the mental models should marketers put into their mental toolbox? There are quite a few to work with, but to help us be more effective, we are just going to take a look at some of the top options including.

Anchoring Bias

This mental model is going to talk about the phenomenon where people are going to rely heavily on the first piece of information that comes their way and will use this information to base and make future assumptions. Let's say that you have a pair of shoes in the store, and the customer asks you how much it is going to cost. You quote a price of $99, and the customer makes a counteroffer of $75. You request them to meet you a bit higher and they make a final offer of $80 when you accept the deal.

The customer is going to walk away feeling that they were able to get a good deal. But the trick is that you would have been just fine if you sold it for $60. The customer made a counteroffer based on the $80. If you told them the shoes were for $60, there is no way they would have offered $80, and you would have probably had to sell them for $50 or something lower.

This means that as a marketer, the first piece of information that you are able to provide to a customer is going to help lead here their subsequent assumptions are going to go with a product. This is why you want to make sure that the very first piece of information that you provide to them is the one that you want to stick in their minds.

Loss Aversion

Naturally, most people like to avoid loss. There are very few people who are going to deliberately desire to lose unless the cost of gaining is extremely high compared to the cost of losing. Psychologists have found that people are going to prefer it if they are able to avoid losses rather than acquiring an equivalent gain. For example, most people would rather not lose

$100 rather than gain the $100. If they had a chance to win $100 but there was an equal chance of losing that same amount of money, then most of the time, people are going to walk away from the opportunity.

Every marketer, especially when they are trying to get into a new market, is going to use loss aversion as one of their marketing strategies. The marketer is going to try to craft up their own strategy that can help eliminate that sense of loss in the mind of the customer so that the customer is more likely to choose this product over one of the others.

Product/Market Fit

A market is simply a place where the supply is going to meet with demand. The demand that we are talking about here is going to be the expression of the wants and needs of the customer. The product is simply a solution that is devised in order to satisfy the wants of the customers. This means that in a product/market fit, it is going to be the situation where a supplier's product is going to be the best fits a customer's demand. In essence, a solution that is best going to fit the given need.

This kind of model is going to work because it encourages businesses to seek to gain a better understanding of the wants and needs of the consumer, before developing any products. If this doesn't happen, then the business is going to run a higher risk of the product failing to meet the market or the needs of the consumer.

Traditionally, a company would try to create a product and hope that it was successful enough that the market would want it, and they could make a lot of money. This could end up being really costly though because the market may have no use for the product, and then the business is out a lot of money in the process.

Mental Models for Financiers and Accountants

Financiers and accountants are going to find that they rely quite a bit on these mental models, especially the ones that are designed by economists. Economists are probably only rivaled by the field of psychology when it comes to generating some of these mental models, which means that the people in this group are going to have a lot of different mental models that they are able to rely on to help them get work done.

Even with this in mind, we will only take the time to consider a few of the mental models that are available for this group. Our goal is to focus on the mental models that are generally applicable and won't be confined to just their professional domains, even though these business individuals are going to be able to use these models in a variety of manners. Some of the different mental models that are perfect and helpful for those who are financiers and accountants are going to include:

Compounding

The first mental model that we are going to look at is known as compounding. This model is going to look at each new earning as an income stream. For example, if you have an investment of $100 and you earn 10 percent in interest, which is $10, this is going to become $10 of a new income stream. And it keeps compounding on itself over and over again to help you make more money.

This is the simplest form of compounding in the world of financing and accounting and of course, there are other, more complicated methods that you are able to use as well. But one of the most important things that you have to remember about the compounding mental model is that it is going to help a financier and an accountant of the potential worth of every new income stream.

Sunk Cost

A sunk cost is going to be any kind of cost that occurs that can't be redeemed at all. This means that the cost is going to be irreversible. The sunk cost model is going to remind people in this kind of group that they have to be more conscious of the ways they are incurring and expending their costs. Some sunk costs can't be avoided, but it is important to limit this as much as possible so that money is not wasted.

Since the sunk cost is something that we are not able to recover later on, accountants are often advised that it is best to write these off. This is a much better thing to do than to laboriously keep them on the record, which is sometimes going to affect the true financial position of that company and could really negatively affect the quality of decisions that are made.

The danger that comes with not writing off these sunk costs is that it could consume more costs down the line. for example, following up on a bad debt can end up being very costly. There is going to be a point in time when the cost-benefit is not going to work out, and you spend more money on that debt that it was worth to get paid. When it becomes more expensive to try and recover the bad debt, rather than just writing it off, then this is not a good thing.

Opportunity Cost

The opportunity cost is going to be the benefit of the next best alternative that has been sacrificed to get where you are. In a real-world scenario, we are going to be confronted with a lot of choices, and we have to decide on just one choice over all the others.

Let's say that you forego a job that is going to pay you $18 an hour in order to take up a job that is going to pay you $20 an hour. The opportunity cost of the chosen job is going to be $19. Thus, comparing the two jobs, you have made a net gain of $2 per hour. The $2 an hour is going to be the actual pay that you will get above the opportunity cost.

Many times, we are tempted to make some decisions without taking the time to factor in the opportunity cost of that decision. Then we eventually realize that we should have factored this in, or we would have picked a different choice than the one we went with.

The Time Value of Money

Another mental model that is popular is going to be the time value of money. This is actually seen as one of the most important concepts when it comes to the fields of accounting, finance, and economics. What you have at the moment could end up being worth more than what you expect to have at some point in the future. As such, you can't equate what you have right now against a similar value in the future.

The time value of money is what is going to account for things like depreciation, interest rates, and inflation rates in the accounting world. Using the idea of the compounding model that we talked about earlier, it is easier to see that $100 now can't be the same as it will be ten years from now. If this $100 is factored with a 10 percent compound interest rate per year, in 10 years' time, this is going to be quite a bit of money due to the multiple income streams that are earned with the interest compound.

This means also that if you lend someone $100 and they promise to pay it back in ten years, such as with an endowment plan, retirement benefits, and pension, you have to ask yourself what it is worth now. Knowing what that money is worth right now is going to help you to avoid a new opportunity cost that is higher than the promise they are giving.

Another thing that we have to keep in mind here is that we have income as a factor of time. income is just the rate of dollar flow per a given interval. This could be per second, per hour, per month and so on. When we are able to put this all together, we will see that all of this makes it easier for an accountant to calculate out a lot of things such as how much it costs when employees are absent or late, the cost of moonlighting and more. Then they can take this information and tell the business how much it is losing every second an employee is out of work and not doing what they were supposed to do.

The Pyramid Model

When we take a look at the world of accounting, the pyramid model is going to be used to group together accounts that are pretty simple. For example, there are going to often bet three main classes of accounts when we are in accounting and these include Liabilities, Capital, and Assets. Most of the money and how it is used in the company will ensure that it fits into one of those three categories along the way.

All accounts related to transfer, decrease, or increase the assets are going to just be grouped together into one class that is known as Assets to make it easier. In a similar manner, all of the accounts that are going to record the transfer, decrease, or increase of capital in any form will be grouped under the category of Capital Account. And finally, all of the accounts that are related back to a transfer, decrease, or increase of liabilities will be added to the Liabilities account.

This is done in order to make things flow together a little bit easier. If we tried to put them into all of those accounts, in this case about nine different ones, the accounts, and the charts that you use to monitor all of these, are going to get full pretty quickly, and it is going to be difficult to figure out what is going on. When they are grouped together in just those three categories, it makes the job of your accountant so much easier to work with.

In this case with finances and accounting, the pyramid model is going to be used in a manner to help organize all of the accounting information so that it is in a more systematic way, making it easier to interpret, analyze, and read before making decisions based on the business performance. If this information is in order, then we have a much better look at how the business is performing based on its financial transactions, and it is much easier to make the changes that are needed.

Accountants and financiers have to spend a lot of time looking at numbers, transactions, and more to ensure that a business is doing well and that they are not headed for disaster. Even with this in mind, there are a lot of mental models that can come into play to help you get things done and to ensure that you will be able to get the work done effectively, and with no mistakes along the way!

Mental Models for Business Entrepreneurs

Now that we have had a chance to look at some of the mental models that can work for marketers, it is time to take a look at some of the different mental models that we are able to work with as business entrepreneurs.

Entrepreneurship is one area where you will find mental models really aiding when it is time to come up with novel solutions that can change society and make a big impact. Some of the different mental models that work for business entrepreneurs well include:

The Idea Maze

This mental model is going to warn against rushing over an idea without doing the due consideration ahead of time, and without making sure that you know the exit point. There are a lot of entry points that can come with a maze. It is important that you don't just focus on these, but you also consider the exit point of all the entries before you invest money, time, and effort into that channel. If you don't, then it is possible that you will get trapped and have no exit except to head to your entry, and this can result in a huge loss.

The Idea maze is going to caution one to consider that one of the ideas that you have may not be unique. Consider others who have gone through with similar ideas and how they invested their energy and time. Then consider if they were successful with their work or not. This way, you can make sure to save your business by not getting entangled into a death trap that already caught someone else earlier on.

The idea that comes with this one is that it encourages a potential startup to ventilate enough of its ideas first, before using them, by simply exposing it to others so that the opinions and views of those others can be weighed into it as well. It is going to try and discourage the desire by most startups to hold onto the idea with the thought that if they try to share their ideas, then the idea will get stolen.

The Problem Hypothesis

This is going to be another example of a mental model where you are going to try and reframe your great idea around some kind of problem that you are able to test and validate. This means that your idea is going to turn into something that can solve a given problem. Some things to consider with this one include:

1. The problem has to be one that actually exists.
2. There is no better solution to solving the problem, outside of your idea.
3. That your idea can generate a Minimum Viable Product (we will talk about this in the next mental model).

The problem hypothesis is going to help you to avoid some of the pitfalls that are common that many upcoming entrepreneurs are going to face, which is that they try to create a solution to a problem that does not exist. Because of this, the solution is going to fail to gain traction in the market, as there is no real need case. This mental model is going to require that you work with the scientific approach to validate all of your ideas before you actually try to use any of them in your business.

Minimum Viable Product

Another mental model that you can work with to ensure that your business is a success is the minimum viable product. This is simply going to be a product that has just the very basic of features to satisfy early adopters and can provide the creators of the product with some feedback about the real needs of the market. this feedback can be used in such a way that it helps to guide some of the future development of that product.

It is hard for a lot of potential entrepreneurs to come up with a complex final product, and spend all that time, money and effort on it, just to find out that it doesn't meet the product/market fit criteria. They may lose out with this one because the product is not really what the consumer is looking for, for a variety of reasons, and they are not able to make any money from it.

Instead of letting the risk of that happen, the Minimum Viable Product is going to be a model that is going to require a lot of little changes to the product, based on the feedback that you get from the market. you start out with a product that has just the basic features and the fundamentals that make it work. From there, you wait to get some feedback before deciding which direction to take the product, what new features to add and more.

This helps with decision making. You don't have to worry about making the wrong decisions any longer because the consumer is basically making them for you. And you don't have to risk things as much, or waste as much time, but the changes that you make are small, and then you can release the product again, make some money in the process, and then bring it back in for some more changes based on some of the new feedback that you hear from your customer along the way.

Mental models for CEO and Managers

The next part of the business that we need to talk about in terms of mental models is going to be the ones that work well for chief executives, managers, and even supervisors. These are the individuals who have to deal with a lot of challenges when it comes to running a company, making sure they meet the needs of the consumer, and training and leading their employees. Because of this, they are going to have a lot of things on their plates, and there are a few mental models that work well for them as well. Some of the best options for mental models that can work for CEO's and other managerial positions will include the following:

Casual Loop

The casual loop model is going to be able to help us see the cause and effect relationship that happens between the various components of a system. This is going to help us see the impact of changing one of the variables on the system as a whole. The reason that many managers like to use this is that it allows them to see how their decisions will affect what kind of outcome they are going to get. For example, they may be weighing the impact of shifting from monthly salary to hourly wage to see how it is going to influence the morale of the workers and their productivity in the process.

Reversible vs. Irreversible Decisions

This kind of decision model is going to be one that you can use to categorize decisions into those that can be undone, and the ones that you are not able to be undone. For example, if you purchase a product that has a return period, then this is something that is reversible. On the other hand, if you fire an employee, this is something that is usually not reversible because it is not very prudent and can make things difficult.

Working with this kind of model will enable a manager to re-evaluate the likely impact of their decisions before they try to execute them, and this helps them to see in a clearer picture what is really at stake for each of these decisions. The reversible decisions are going to be the ones that have the lower stakes compared to the irreversible decisions. This makes it imperative that you put more of the thought energy has to be allocated to evaluating the likely impact of the irreversible decisions.

And to help reduce some of the stakes that you are seeing, you want to make sure that you turn as many contracts and as many decisions into reversible ones as possible. This allows you to create some escape routes if they are needed. This is why some companies are going to hire an employee and will work with extended probation, short term contracts, freelancing, and more.

The Pyramid Model

The pyramid model is going to mainly be one for the Chief Executive or some of the top managers who are going to design the organization structure. In this kind of model, the related functions are going to be grouped together with one department or division. This means that at the top, there is only going to be one group that can break down into several groups as it goes down and each group is going to break down into more groups until you get to the smallest group possible in the end.

99/50/1

This is a model that is going to be suited the best for supervisors. The core part of this model is that you have to follow up when a task has just begun and then again when it is about 99 percent complete. This is done to ensure that the people who are assigned the responsibility of doing this task are actually working on it, and they are doing it in the right manner.

Afterward, you can check again when the task is close to 50 percent complete. This is going to be done in order to confirm that it is substantially done and that you can then anticipate when the completion time is going to happen. And then the final leg of this is going to be that the supervisor should check when the project is just about done, or when there is about 1 percent remaining. This ensures that you are there to help out and check on the finishing of the project and the wrap-up of everything.

Each of these mental models are going to help you whether you are marketing for a company, trying to be the head of the company and you want to make sure you are providing a product that the consumer actually wants, and when you are one of the supervisors who want to check that you are going to get things done on time. Working with the right mental model can make it so that decision making is effective, fast, and accurate as much as possible.

Chapter 6: Writing and Inquisitive? The Best Mental Models to Help You

Investigators, inquisitors, journalists, and writers all have one thing in common with each other. They like to establish facts and then report these facts for some kind of action. In this chapter, we are going to take a look at these mental models and how they can be used to help those who are involved in establishing facts from stories, allegations, insinuations and other kinds of information to achieve their very important missions as effectively as possible.

The Socratic Questioning Technique

This is going to be a mental model that has been devised in order to inspire some critical thinking along the way. This technique is going to employ a set of questions that will enable someone to learn about their own fallacies, their unfounded assumptions, and limiting beliefs. And by this discovery, the person is going to be able to think in a more critical manner. You will continue to work with this one until you can come up with the right answer that makes the most sense of the situation.

The Why Iteration

The next mental model that we are going to take a look at is known as the Why iteration. This one is going to be where you ask the why question five times at a minimum. The point of this one is that you want to get to the root of the initial response, rather than stopping at some superficial point along the way. the assumption with the Why Iteration is that the first response is rarely the final one, and relying on this first response is not going to give you the true picture of things that you need. Here we see that the more questions we ask, the closer we can get to the root of the matter.

You are able to consider each Why in order to address a specific layer in the structure. And you also have to consider the problem as a type of root that has five layers down. The first why that you ask is going to be able to address the respective portion of the root in the first layer, but there are four other portions and four other layers that you need to spend some time on before fully understanding the problem.

One thing to keep in mind with this one is that the 5 is not really empirical, but more of an encouragement.

Some structures could have fewer numbers, and others are going to have more. But don't use this as an excuse to just ask why two times and give up. Work at adding in as many different layers to the problem as you can, and see what a difference it can make.

The NLP Meta Model

The NLP Meta Model is going to be similar to the Socratic model that we talked about before. It is going to help us to make some deep inquiries into information that may not be availed by word labels. What a person says is often just a small percentage of the entire information that is held by that person, basically just the tip of the iceberg. It is not always the intent of the other person to filter out the information, but they may do it to shorten up the conversation if needed or to just give you their perception of the most important information. In the process of perceiving information from a sensory organ, the brain:

1. Deletes a bit of the sensory information to make it easier to do the processing.

2. Distorts part of the sensory information based on what experiences you have had in the past.

3. Generalizes the sensory information, especially if the information was really repetitive in nature.

All of these are going to be done in an endeavor to effectively utilize the limited space in the memory, to fit the existing mental models, and to prioritize the functional benefits a bit. Thus, to help us get a clear picture, we need to ask some specific questions that we can recycle or reconstruct the deleted portion of the message, to straighten out the part that is distorted, and unwrap some of the generalizations so that e can get more information out of this person. A good example of what this is going to look like when we work with the NLP model includes:

1. Distortion: I am pretty sure that he is feeling jealous, I am sure that his congratulation message is not genuine.

2. Deletion: No one likes seeing me successful. When people tell me they do, it's always a fake compliment.

3. Generalization: All women are gold-diggers.

From the statements above, you can see that there is so much information that we are missing out on and that is being withheld from this. Using the NLP meta model, you will be able to ask a specific set of questions to that other person in order to figure out what is at the root of that statement. This one is also a good option to use in therapies because it gives you the ability to understand the problems of others better, or to help them to understand their own problems in a deeper manner.

The Response Bias

Response bias is going to occur where an interviewee is going to give a response that is not really based on the facts, but it is more based on some of the other factors that are nearby. It could include some factors like the desire to please, fear, a desire to look politically or socially correct, a desire to conform, and even a desire to avoid telling the other person the truth.

Because of this bias, researchers, journalists and more need to learn how to not overly rely on a given response without putting it to strict empirical test and proof. You want to make sure that you are getting the right answers from others, rather than getting this bias that is going to distort the kind of image that you are able to get from the other person. If you can learn how to take away some of the bias, and get the other person to feel more comfortable and open around you, you may find that they will give you better answers, without the bias, and this can do some wonders in the process.

Even someone who has more of an inquisitive mind and who wants to be able to get to the root of the problem and find all of the facts will be able to use some of the mental models that we discuss in this guidebook. Learning how to use these, when to use these, and the best time to pull each one out is going to ensure that you find the results that you ant as well.

Chapter 7: Improving Your Parenting with Mental Models

Parenting can be tough. We have to work at raising small children who, even though they rely on us for a lot of things, and need us to care for them and watch out for them, have their own personalities and their own way of viewing the world. They won't share the same thoughts and feelings as us, mainly because they are children and are going to have a different way of viewing the world, and partly because they may have different personalities than us.

In addition to the basics of raising these children, we also have to focus on a lot of other topics. We have to worry about which daycare to use, which school, how to balance family time, work time, and time in activities. We worry about their friends and what they are learning along the way. There is just so much to keep track of and worry about when it comes to being a parent, whether you have one child or many.

Parenting is often seen as one of the most challenging professions in the world. Yet it is not really going to get a ton of attention when it comes to the formal schooling ideas. Because of this, it is found that very few scholars are going to bother to device an appropriate methodology for parenting and even coming up with the best mental models to help parents out.

This doesn't mean that you are stuck without any kind of mental model. We just need to be a bit creative here to find the answers that we need. Thanks to the diversity that comes with social orientations, environments, and cultures it is sometimes hard to find a uniform methodology, and therefore a universal mental model, that is going to be tailored to parenting.

Nonetheless, we can come up with some of the mental models that are already around, and use that in a customizable way to help fit the parenting role across societal orientations, environments, and cultures. We are going to take a look at some of the different mental models that you are able to follow that can help you to make parenting a little bit easier to handle.

Regret Minimization

As a parent, you may find that there are things that you regret. You may regret that you did not spend enough time with the kids during the day. You may regret that you have to run errands rather than hanging out and relaxing. You may even regret the activities that you signed your children up in. but with this mental model, we are going to embrace regret minimization as much as possible.

The first thing to like about the regret minimization mental model is that it is going to help you to reflect on how you would like to see your children being once they turn into adults. As such this can help you to raise them in a manner that will ensure they become responsible adults when they grow up.

Regret minimization is also going to work from the side of the children. In what way or manner would you like your children to perceive you once they are grown u? DO you want them to see you as a great parent who went to great lengths to ensure that their childhood as well lived? Or are you fine with them seeing you as not wroth them as a result of the suffering that you inflicted on them due to abuse, neglect, and abandonment?

Of course, most of us want to go with the first option, and regret minimization will help you to learn the best method to use to minimize the regret as much as possible. You can use this to pick the course of action that is going to cause you the least amount of regret. For example, are you going to regret the dishes sitting there a bit longer, or the time you missed out playing with the kids? Yes, you do need to clean the house on occasion, but putting the dishes off until the kids go to bed rather than doing them right now may help you to minimize regret, while getting to spend more time with your kids.

There are a lot of things in life that can cause you to regret. You aren't able to avoid all of them, no matter how much you may wish that you were able to do so. But when it comes to being the best parent possible to your child, learning how to limit the regret as much as you can will really make a world of difference to the results that you are able to get.

When making any decision regarding your child, don't waste a lot of time thinking through a list of pros and cons. Think about how much regret you will have doing one action over another, or the regret that you will have if you decide not to do the action at all. And then make your decisions based on this in the first place.

Compounding

The next type of mental model that we are going to take a look at is the idea of compounding. Every effort that you put into the process of raising each child is going to compound. Imagine with this one that a little bit of effort spent on your children whether it is helping them with a project, taking them to an activity, making them lunch, or playing with them, is going to have a profound effect on them for the rest of their lives.

It doesn't have to be a ton of effort or even a lot of time. Ten minutes spending time with them, rather than viewing your phone and social media, can really add up and compound with this mental model. Your children are going to remember you, and they are more likely to do the same things with their children, and it continues on down the line. All because of the simple actions that you were able to take with them today.

Imagine some of the simple words and terms that you try to teach your baby? Even though you start out small and don't overwhelm them with new information, these simple terms are going to build up into a language that they can use to communicate with those around them. And then they can use these terms to teach their own children and so on.

What you do to your children is going to end up with a compound effect on the entire generation. You can change up this entire generation by simply changing up the way that you bring up your own children. A child who has been raised well is going to become the foundation of a healthy new generation, so keep this in mind.

You may sometimes feel that your efforts are in vain and that you are doing a lot of work that is not noticed or appreciated at all. But this is not the case. In fact, just a bit of your time, given over a consistent basis, can make a world of difference in the lives of your children. Take some time to spend with them, rather than overthinking things or worrying about all of the household things you need to get done, and you will find that it can really help you out.

Think of how amazing it is going to be when you can imagine your actions as compounding not just with your children, but with your grandchildren, your great-grandchildren and on down the line! A simple act of spending time with your children, and giving them the love and attention that they need and ant can really compound into the future.

The 10/10/10 rule

The next kind of mental model that we need to be able to focus on is going to be the 10/10/10 rule. This one is going to be based on the idea of foresight. You simply need to ask yourself the following questions below involving the interval of 10. Let's look at the questions:

1. How will I feel about it in ten minutes?
2. How will I feel about this in ten months?
3. How will I feel about this in ten years?

As you can guess, this will work with a lot of different aspects of your life, and not just with child-raising. But it is a good way to really put things in perspective in life and can help you to not sweat the little things, while also enjoying some of the little things along the way as well.

For example, when your kid spills milk on the floor, you can bring in this mental model. Think about how you will feel about this spill in ten minutes. Yes, you may still feel a bit upset about it, and that is fine. But how are you going to feel in ten months? This is probably as far as you are going to need to go with this one because by then, you won't even remember the spill because it was such a small and insignificant part of your life. If it isn't going to matter to you in ten months or ten years then it is something that you can just let go and not worry so much about.

Let's look at this another way. As a parent, you will remember all of those long and sleepless nights, holding the baby and being kept awake. You were tired, and worn out, and thought it would never end. Let's use this principle here. In ten minutes, you're still going to be tired and hoping the baby will go to sleep so you can get some sleep and not feel so tired.

But how about in ten months? Likely the baby will be out of this phase, and while there may be a few times you get up at night, you won't be sitting in the rocking chair and holding them, and you won't be sleepless as much. At this point, you may feel grateful that you get a good nights' sleep and like you are able to parent a little bit better.

But what about in ten years? With this one, the child is probably 10 or 11. They have their own friends, spend their day in school, and have the activities that they like to do on their own. They won't be your little baby anymore, just wanting to snuggle in your arms and have you hold them. At ten years, you may find that you miss the snuggles and the closeness that you once had with your child.

This is a good way to keep some of the hard things in parenting in perspective. It helps you to realize that your time as a parent is going to be short. Yes, you will always love them and always be their parent, but being the one responsible for everything for your child is going to come to an end sooner than you know. Keeping these thoughts, and the 10/10/10 rule in mind can help you keep it all in order and keep yourself feeling better about the whole ordeal.

This is also a good one to use on some of your own personal development as well because it helps you to put things into perspective and realize all of the good things that you have in your life. Whether you are going to use it in parenting or for your own happiness and personal development (and it can work well with both, to be honest), you will find that the 10/10/10 rule is going to be a great option to use.

The Pareto 80/20 Rule

We talked about the Pareto rule a bit before, but now we are going to look at it from the view of parenting and how we are able to use this for helping us to raise good and smart children along the way. The Pareto 80/20 rule is going to apply to parenting, as it does to a few of the other methods that we have talked about in this guidebook.

This rule is going to talk about how just 20 percent of the efforts of the parent was going to contribute to 80 percent of the lifetime gain of the child, while about 80 percent is going to contribute to only 20 percent of this same kind of gain.

Educating a child, especially for a parent who is busy and working, while keeping up with all of the other things that they need to handle, can be one of the least efforts but it is going to contribute to the biggest lifetime gain of your child. Don't count education or school to do this. This can never, and will never, match that kind of education that a parent is able to impart over to their own children.

While focusing on education can be important, you want to make sure that you are focusing on a few other options as well. This can include play, a good amount of healthcare (such as taking them to their doctor appointments), and a healthy and balanced diet. They are easily going to fall into the twenty percent effort that can be provided by the parent but they are really going to provide the child with a ton of great benefits.

The Pareto rule advises parents to focus as much of their energy on this 20 percent rather than on things that may seem important, but really are not. This ensures that you are not running around doing a lot of things that don't really matter in the long run, while helping you to give your children the highest lifetime heritage possible.

The Expert Generalist

The final mental model that we are going to take a look at is the expert generalist. If there is any field where being a specialist is a disability to how well you do, then parenting would be it. When it comes to the world of parenting, you have no choice other than learning how to be an expert generalist if you want to be good at everything.

As one of these expert generalists, you have to be a bit of everything. Parents are a wonderful mix of a dressmaker, lab technician, psychologist, games coach, security guard, mechanic, teacher, nurse, nutritionist, daycare provider and more. Your child is going to prove to be a big challenge for you in all of these, and it is impossible for you to learn how to be an expert in all of them.

This may mean that while your job will demand you to be a specialist to bring home a check being a parent demands that you become a generalist. You don't have to know everything, which can be a great relief to parents trying to do it all. But knowing enough to keep up with the rapidly changing moods, preferences, motion, tastes, and growth of your child can be enough to become a great parent to them.

Parenting is going to be a challenge. Each child is going to be different, and often they have their own minds and want things to go their way, not the way the parent wants. When we add in all of the other obligations and challenges that parents face along the way in trying to raise these children, it can become hard to get things done and make sure that you are being the good and loving parent that you want to be.

This is why mental models can be used here to help make a difference. The mental models that we have talked about in this chapter are meant to help you make the right decisions for you and your children, and to show you that you are more than likely doing a better job with parenting than you had thought!

Chapter 8: Mental Models for Educators and Critical Thinkers

Critical thinkers, psychotherapists, and educators are all going to come with one thing in common, they are going to be actively concerned when it comes to the methodology that is used for knowing, acting, and perceiving. The good news is that even this group of individuals will be able to work with some of the mental models to help them see some of the results that they want in critical thinking and decision making.

Mental Models of Perceiving, Acting, and Knowing

Often, we are going to see things, not really for what they are, but as we are. We are able to create a reality in our minds. And without the mind, we are not going to have any reality. Without the mind, there is not going to be a world, and in essence, there is no view of the world. It is common for a lot of us to confuse the world and the earth. On a larger scale, we are going to confuse the world with the universe. These are different topics, but basically, the world is just going to be a mental model of how we are able to perceive nature, the nature of beings and the nature of things. As such, the world is going to be a kind of mental model on its own.

With that in mind, it is time for us to take a look at some of the different mental models that you are able to use when it comes to working with mental models for critical thinkers and educators.

The Cognitive Bias

This mental model is going to be an error in reasoning that is able to deviate the decision-maker from making any deductions that are rational. To some extent, we will find that the cognitive bias that we have is going to be a completely natural phenomenon. It is simply the way that the brain is going to work. Often it is going to be a very complex process for the brain to work through each and every piece of information that reaches it from all of our senses, from touch, taste, sound, eyes, and more.

This is just too much energy and our mind is not able to give full attention to all of the aspects that are a part of our existence. Because of this, there is going to be some form of cognitive bias to help make sure that the brain knows which information to focus on, and which to avoid. There is just not enough energy or resources in the brain to handle everything, and it would end up driving us all insane in the process to try this, so the cognitive bias helps us to utilize, in the most effective manner possible, the limited amount of resources and energy that are available.

Keep in mind here that there are going to be a few kinds of cognitive biases that are not seen as natural. These are going to be created out of a few different things, like misinformation and parental nurturing, schooling, traditional practices, and more. It is unnatural to have these kinds of cognitive biases and if you realize that these are things you are dealing with, then it is something that you do have to confront early on.

It is important to note that critical thinking is something that you will not be able to use to the optimal level if you are controlled by this cognitive bias. Yet, it is through the critical thinking process that you will be able to debunk most of these biases in the first place. For this to happen, the mental models will become of primary essence as an external source of reinforcement against your cognitive bias in the first place.

The Socrative Dialogue

The next kind of mental model that we are going to look at is the Socratic dialogue. This is going to be the most commonly applied critical thinking models when you want to go through an intellectual discourse. With this method, instead of directly criticizing someone or telling them, in a blunt manner, that their statement is wrong, and thus pushing the other person to feel attacked and like they need to go on the defensive, you are able to work with the Socratic dialogue in order to ask a set of questions so that the other person, rather than yourself, is going to make the inquiry to themselves.

With the help of this self-inquiry, the person will then be able, on their own, to come to their own conclusions, often to the idea that the statement they put up is not factual, and that they have some naked beliefs, assumptions, and fallacies that they need to be able to work on.

Since you were able to prompt the person to go through this self-inquiry, rather than pushing them into it and making them defensive, you are assisting the person in actually thinking through things, rather than being lazy and accepting things. When this is able to continue, the person is going to gain the habit of making this kind of inquiry into themselves before they come up with any statements in the future.

Of course, you don't have to use this mental model just on other people. You can use this as a dialogue within. Before you hold onto a position, ask yourself some pertinent questions about this position, as if someone else were holding onto it. This way, you can get rid of the assertions with no basis, the baseless assumptions, the unwarranted beliefs, the cognitive biases, and even some of the matters that may be held in your concept, but which are not actually factual or adding to it.

These are the main models that work for those in this kind of category. Some of the others that you can consider if these don't seem like the right ones for you to use include:

1. The Fifth Discipline
2. Abundance Mentality vs. Scarce Mentality
3. Defensive Reasoning
4. Contagion Anxiety
5. Causal Attribution

Chapter 9: Using Mental Models to Help You to Be Happy and In Personal Development

Now that we have had some time to look into some of the different mental models that you are able to work with in other aspects of your life, it is time to take a look at some of the mental models that you can use to increase your happiness and help with personal development.

Americans and others throughout the world spend hundreds of dollars, if not more, each year working with personal development classes, training events books, and other options. But instead of doing that, we can simply work with a mental model and change our lives around. It is such a simple idea, and it is likely that these mental models are going to be similar, and just as easy, as the ones that we have already been able to discuss in this guidebook so far.

In the human sphere, it is all going to begin in our own individualism, before things can spread out into relationships between these individuals. Because of this, personal development is going to take a central role when it comes to first improving the individuality of a person, and then spreading out the benefits that come with that improvement to the rest of their relationships with friends and family members.

We have already been able to consider the effects of the FMM AND and the FMM OR mental models earlier in this guidebook. Each of these is important and can be beneficial, as long as they are used to balance one another out. Do not forget these as you work to reach your own personal development.

If either of the FMM is out of order or one becomes stronger than the others, this can be a problem. It results in us getting out of control, taking over, using our ideas to influence others in a negative manner, or, on the other side, letting others take full advantage of us in the process.

In this chapter, we are going to take a look at a few more of the mental models that you are able to utilize in your own life to see some great results. These are going to ensure that you are able to reach the happiness that you are looking for, while also promoting your own personal development in the process. So, let's get started!

Mental Models for Personal Development

The Circle of Competence

The first mental model that we are going to take a look at when it comes to being happy and working on your own personal development is the Circle of Competence. You can't have complete knowledge of all the spheres in the world. You can't be skilled and talented in all of the fields and all of the talents out there. it is just impossible so why waste our time and our energy trying?

Because of this, it is important to learn ahead of time what we can do, and who we are! It is important to acknowledge where you are not fit and seek to develop some of the core areas where you are really at your best and where you are able to shine.

The Circle of Competence is going to be important when it comes to a lot of different spheres of your life, but specifically when it comes to your career choice, and in developing your career. Choose one or a few areas where you are able to do really well, and outshine others in that field, and then focus on just doing that and showing that off in your job.

This does not mean that you are going to overlook, neglect, or ignore the areas that are on the fringes of your life and where you are not the most competent in. Over time, as you are developing more of your skills you can gradually extend the boundaries of your skills and knowledge so that you can add to your core competence. This way, you will be able to avoid the common disability of being too wide and shallow, or even of being too deep and narrow.

But width, as well as depth, are going to be important, so you need to be able to balance these optimally. What is even more important here is that you need to be able to build up a mutually beneficial mastermind alliance with those who are already specialists in your fringes. This helps you to form some new relationships and can cover you in these areas where you are falling a bit, all at the same time and in the process.

Parkinson's Law

The next thing that we need to look at is the Parkinson's Law. This one is often brought up in human resource type positions or personalities, but we are still going to take a moment to look at it here. This mental model can work well with some of the personal development that you may want to do in the process as well, so it is time to take a look at it here.

The greatest challenge that can come with personal development is how you are able to manage your time in a manner so that you can be more effective with it. This helps you get more done in a smaller amount of time while helping to boost up the amount of productivity that you are experiencing on a regular basis.

You will find that there are a lot of tools out there that are going to work with this mental model. These tools sometimes work, and sometimes don't, but they are meant to help you really manage your time to get more done in the process. Often the one that you go with is going to depend on your own personal preferences and what works the best to motivate you. Some of the tools that have been devised to help you work with the Parkinson's Law mental model will include the critical path method, time Scheduler, Gantt Charts, To-Do Lists, and the Pomodoro Timer.

The Parkinson's law is not meant to be overly difficult, and you may find that it is easier to work with than you would think. Some of the steps that you can take to make sure you can properly utilize this kind of mental model for your personal development includes:

1. Take a look at the tasks that you need to do and then break the tasks up into achievable chunks.

2. Allocate the chunks that you made into a specific completion time.

3. Schedule performance of each chunk using any or some of the above-mentioned tools and narrowing the time margins between each chunk so that there is some error of safety if needed. You can pick the one that you want to use in terms of methods, but make sure that at least one is in place to help you with this.

4. Be dedicated and disciplined so that you make sure you stick with the method and the

schedule that you have set up and get the work done quickly and efficiently.

Mental Models for Personal Happiness

We just looked at a few of the mental models that you are able to use to help with personal development. Now we are going to take it a bit further and look at some of the mental models that you can use to help reach your own personal happiness including tranquility, joy, peace, and satisfaction.

Happiness is a term that is sometimes hard to define, yet its feeling is such an easy one to express. Because of this, there isn't really going to be a standard that is universal when we look at happiness. Each person, culture, country and more will have their own ideas on happiness and what it entails. Even with this though, we all know what it feels like to be happy.

We also have a good idea that happiness is going to be in the mind. There can be two people in similar circumstances, and one is happy and the other is not. This is why having the right mental model in place can help to condition us, and our happiness levels will go through the roof. Just by learning how to condition our minds, we will learn that happiness can be found anywhere and that we don't have to spend time searching for it any longer.

There are several mental models that you are able to use that can help you to work on increasing your own personal happiness. Let's take a look at some of these mental models and how they are going to have a direct impact on your own happiness.

Entropy

Entropy is going to be a term that is borrowed from the Second Law of Thermodynamics. To keep it simple, this term is going to state that in a closed system, there is some tendency of the elements that are inside of that system to start moving towards a state of disorder. In our lives, no matter how hard we try and no matter if we give our best efforts or not, there is always going to be a few things that will go wrong. For example, no matter how healthy you try to eat, how much you try to stay active and avoid risks, you will still eventually pass on to the next world.

This model is helpful because it is going to help us to understand that at some level you are going to have disorganization. This is something that is inevitable. Some things just occur randomly, that is, we can work to plan out as much as possible, but the unexpected can always sneak back in and ruin all of those best efforts. We can plan for a big party, but someone will get sick someone will be late, or something else will go wrong in the process.

In some ways, we can look at the entropy model as the ideas that are found in Murphy's Law. This one talks about "anything that can go wrong, will go wrong!" This may seem a bit pessimistic, and we are not saying that you should always assume that everything is going to fail and crash around you. And you are not meant to use this to surrender yourself to fate.

On the contrary, this entropy model is going to state that we need to keep on the process of ordering things, organizing ourselves, and improving ourselves each and every moment to rise above this disorder state, the state of disintegration, and the state of disorganization. For example, you should not stop eating healthy and doing physical exercise just because you are going to die anyway. You shouldn't stop taking care of yourself just because you are going to, at some point, get sick anyway.

You have to try and stay on top of the disorder and enjoy your life anyway. When you choose to do nothing, then the rate of decay and disintegration will end up catching on to you. Instead of letting this happen, you will learn how to do something so that you are able to rise above some of the processes that are part of nature, at least do this as much as you possibly can.

The Pratfall Effect

The idea of this mental model is that your likeability is going to increase if you aren't seen as perfect all of the time. it is a common adage that perfectionists are hardly able to live a life that is happy. They are going to torment themselves for mistakes that they made. This should not be the case because we have to remember that mistakes, no matter how hard we try to avoid them are going to be a part of our human nature.

People will feel bad or embarrassed when they make mistakes or do a blunder. Yet you will find that people like you better when you make these mistakes. According to psychologists, perfectionists are hardly likable at all due to their high standards causing discomfort and fear in many. This often causes them to be shunned, and that is not the right step to happiness.

When you are able to show others, and admit to others, that you are not perfect, people are going to start seeing you as more human, more normal, and more approachable rather than some perfect deity that they don't really want to be around. Thus, to help increase your happiness, you need to let go of your fear of making mistakes.

Now, this doesn't mean that you can never make mistakes. In fact, this mental model is going to encourage you to make mistakes and own up to them, because this is what will make you happier. If you do make mistakes, and you will then own up to them, and accept them with grace. Don't be scared to make fun of yourself, poke at yourself, and laugh about mistakes. Overall, this is going to be the push that you need to make yourself more likable, helps you to attract more friends, and feel happier overall.

The Spotlight Effect

You look around and notice that people aren't giving you all that much attention. If this is true, isn't it also true that your mistakes are not being noticed by other people as much as you think? More often than not, we are so focused on our mistakes and some of our weaknesses, that we fail to notice some of the really neat things that we are able to do. We assume that everyone else is noticing these things too, and that makes us anxious and worried and upset overall.

The truth is, most people don't even notice. They are so worried about their own mistakes and problems, they are not paying any attention to yours. More often than not, we are going to get consumed by our own weaknesses and faults that we fail to be happy at all. But deep down we have to learn that we are not unhappy because of our faults, but we are feeling unhappy because we think others are noticing our faults, and that they are judging you.

The neat thing with this mental model though is that when we start to realize that a lot of people are more preoccupied with their own affairs and personal challenges and they don't have much focus left to pay attention to your own faults and defects. It is likely that they don't even notice these things. When you realize that the only person catching on to these mistakes and faults, and no one else even sees them, your life is going to become so much happier.

The idea here is that we need to stop putting these imaginary spotlights into the hands of other people and then having these spotlights point back at us. It is time to just realize that we make mistakes, and it doesn't really matter if other people see them or not.

Pygmalion Effect

The idea with this mental model is that greater expectations are going to drive greater performance. Thus, to make sure that you are able to experience a greater performance like we want to see in our personal life, then we need to set expectations that are higher. Think of your expectations like the ceiling. Yes, you can't jump higher than the ceiling that you set up.

But you can definitely choose the location of the ceiling.

The Pygmalion Effect is going to be the opposite of the Golem Effect. When we look at the Golem Effect, lower expectations lead to lower performance. They are similar ideas, just worked in a different manner. Psychologists assert that there is going to be a positive feedback loop between behavior and belief. If you believe you can achieve, then you will find that you can automatically gain the necessary resources and efforts towards achieving that target.

Maslow's Hierarchy of Needs

It is likely that you have heard about this particular idea, but may be curious as to how this is going to play into helping us to feel happier. Let's take a look at how this is supposed to work. Abraham Maslow is a famous psychologist who came up with what is known as Maslow's Hierarchy of Needs. When we look at this model, all of our needs are going to be grouped into three categories that are pretty broad. These include:

1. Our basic needs

2. Or psychological needs

3. Or self-fulfillment needs

Our basic needs are going to be the needs that we have in order to survive. These can be divided up into two main sub-categories to show us how they work together. The basic needs that are a part of Maslow's Hierarchy of needs will include:

1. Safety needs. These are going to be the needs necessary for one to feel secure. It could be something like protection against enemies and wild animals.

2. Physiological needs: These are going to be our needs for survival including shelter, clothing, food, water, and air.

Once we have been able to meet these needs, then it is time to move on to the psychological needs. You will not be able to meet this second group of needs unless the basic needs are met first. The two main sub-categories that help us to understand the psychological needs include:

1. Esteem needs: This is going to refer to meeting the need to feel having accomplished and achieved a great milestone in some part of our lives. It can be at work, with a goal, at school, and more.

2. Belongingness needs: These are going to include some of the social relationship needs that we have. It may include things like a need for friendship, a need for family, and more.

The self-fulfillment needs are going to be the ones that we are required to have in order to feel like we have reached our highest level of actualization. These can help us to feel happy and content with the life that we have. However, keep in mind that you are not able to reach these needs until the others have been met. This means that you can't reach the highest level of actualization if you haven't been able to meet your need for safety and for food for example, or your need to belong.

While there has been some criticism that comes with the Maslow hierarchy of needs, it is a helpful tool to address our complex needs as humans. Whether you agree with it or not, it helps to break down our needs and explains why we may act in one way or another, and how each individual could be in a different section of this mental model to start with.

This mental model is going to remind us to have a balanced approach to cater to the needs that we have, without accidentally (and sometimes on purpose), alienating and neglecting some. For example, while you strive to reach your basic needs, it is important to not let the other two groups of needs fall to the side and get ignored either.

When of the things that makes this hierarchy so debatable with some is the way that it is going to order out the needs and pick which one is the most important. It is generally believed on this model that you have to reach your basic needs before you can start working on the psychological needs, and that you have to reach this second group of needs before you can achieve your psychological needs.

There are some who believe that this can slow us down and will prevent us from reaching our goals. Our psychological needs are no higher than our basic needs and our self-fulfillment needs are not higher than our psychological needs. These are all needs that we can pursue in any order that we want, and even at the same time. You have to decide which method of attack you would like to use to make these work.

Reaching your own level of happiness and working on self-esteem and other parts of personal development can help out in so many aspects of your life. The mental models that we have discussed in this chapter are going to help you to finally take care of yourself, and reach the level of happiness and contentment that you really deserve.

Chapter 10: Case Studies of Mental Models That Actually Worked!

In this part of our guidebook, we are going to take some time to look at a few successful applications of these mental models, and some of the ways that these can be applied. We are going to take a look at some of the modern and the ancient cases of using these mental models to help leaders and more learn a new way of thinking and get themselves ahead.

The Modern Polymath

The first examples that we are going to take a look at are the modern polymath. When we look at modern conventional wisdom it is going to dictate that the specialization is the best path to take. But despite some of the negative arguments that are out there to the contrary, there are going to be those who decide that they should bear the opportunity cost of acting in an unconventional manner.

While this may not make sense to everyone, those who are considered modern polymaths are going to be a kind of jack of all trades. they want to learn as much about as many different topics as possible, learn on the go, and figure out how to get ahead in different spheres. And it has really worked out well for them. Some examples of successful individuals who are modern polymaths and jack of all trades include:

Charlie Munger

The first example that we are going to take a look at is Charlie Munger. He is known as an expert generalist. He has read widely and channeled the lessons that he learned towards his business empire, an empire that he co-founded with Warren Buffet.

Munger is the brainchild behind the latticework that comes with these mental models. Berkshire Hathaway Inc is known as an international investment company that is going to make sure that all of the investments they do on behalf of premium capitalists. Being widely learned in fields that are not necessarily going to be related back to finance and investment has been helpful because it allows Munger to navigate the company's investment decisions, no matter what environment they are in.

As an international investor, it is important to know that you can't really understand the investment climate that is going on in different jurisdictions and in different parts of the world without understanding some of the basic cultures that are found there. this means that you need to know a bit more than just their money and investments. It is important for you to learn more about their world view, culture, and perspectives when it comes to savings and investment. And this is exactly what Charlie Munger did with his mental model of being an expert generalist.

Elon Musk

The next person that we are going to take a look at is Elon Musk. He is a well-known founder of many different enterprises that are well-known throughout the world. Some have taken off well, and others may not be as well-known, but allowed him to get things done and learn from the experience. Some of the enterprises that Elon Musk is known about includes:

1. Tesla Motors: This is a company that makes high-end tech cars, including driverless cars and electric cars.
2. SolarCity: This is a company that focuses on energy conservation.
3. SpaceX: This is a company for launching space vehicles and space travel.
4. Zip2: This is an online content management company.
5. X.com: This is going to be an online financial management company.
6. Confinity: This is a type of merger that went on with X.com and was then able to build the well-known PayPal that we know and use today.

As you can see with these different business ventures, Elon Musk has been able to voyage across a lot of diverse fields that are not really related to one another. This goes from finance to internet, from automobiles, aeronautics, and everything that is in between. He is a typical example of what is known as a modern polymath. Where would he be now if we did not try to broaden out and work with a lot of different options, and instead chose to work with just internet service technology?

Jack Ma

Jack Ma started out as an English teacher but is more known today as the founder of Alibaba. Like Larry Page, he has anchored the foundation that is his using on academics before he started to work on his own internet business. Alibaba, for those who do not know, is a big e-commerce giant that is going to be similar to Amazon in the eastern hemisphere. Some of the other enterprises that Jack Ma has been able to work on includes:

Alipay: This is a payment platform that is based on the idea of escrow.

AliExpress: This is going to be an online retail giant that allows a business to sell their products to a final consumer, no matter where they are located around the world.

Tmall: This is another example of an e-commerce enterprise, but it is going to be focused more on speakers of Chinese that are found in areas like China, Taiwan, and Hong Kong.

Think about what would have happened if Ma decided to just become a specialist and work with being an English teacher, rather than taking some of his interests to the rest of the world. We would not be able to use the multibillion-dollar enterprise known as Alibaba. And it is true that Jack Ma would not be an international personal brand either.

Jeff Bezos

The final name that we are going to take a look at here in this part of the guidebook is Jeff Bezos. He is mostly known for the venture of his known as Amazon. Although Jeff spent his time studying electronics and computer sciences, he started off working in the sector of finances. He then decided to quit his lucrative job in order to start what was originally an online bookstore, called Amazon.com.

Of course, Amazon became so much more than just an online store to buy books. Amazon has had time to diversify so much beyond books including software, gadgets, and even infrastructures. Just like what we were able to see with Larry Page and Jack Ma, but a bit different than Elon Musk, most of Bezos enterprises are going to bear the brand name of Amazon. Some of these are going to be enterprises that are big enough that they could work on their own, some are products. Some of the different enterprises and products that have become well-known within the world due to Amazon's presence includes:

1. Cloud computing
2. IoT
3. Kindle Digital Publishing: A well-known eBook publishing company
4. The platform for Amazon.com
5. The mental models that these individuals used

Now that we have had some time to look at a few well-known jack of all trades and what they have been able to do with their researching and their work, it is time to take a look at the three mental models that they used in order to get the results that they did. The three mental models that we are able to identify when we look at the names above include:

1. The 5-hour rule
2. The expert generalist
3. The T mental model

First is the T Mental model. This is given its name from the letter T. The ideas that come from this is that someone is going to acquire their knowledge in a horizontal manner, across a diverse number of fields. Then that knowledge is going to be funneled vertically down towards a given core area of specialization. This means that they are going to have one general idea that they want to be a specialist in, but then they will work on a lot of different topics and information to learn as much about that topic as possible.

Next is going to be the Expert generalist. These people are going to be the ones that know a little bit about a lot of topics, rather than a lot about a few topics. This is the natural course that shows up when the entrepreneurs from above work with the T Mental model from before.

And the third option is going to be the five-hour rule. This one is the idea that you should study for five hours a day. most of the expert generalists, as well as the polymaths, are big readers. However, they make sure that they are not reading in a narrow manner. Instead, they are going to read in a wider manner, going over a lot of different disciplines and fields. Most likely, it is this reading habit that can help them become polymaths.

Almost all of the people who fit into this kind of category are going to be ardent readers, and sometimes they would read for more than the five hours that this rule talks about. No matter the case, they not only find time to do the reading, but they are busy people. This means there may be some days when they miss out on the reading, but they still manage to average it out through the week to help them learn as much as possible.

The Big Dreams Garage

The next type of group that we are going to take a look at is the Big Dreams Garage. This one is all about startups that began in the backyard garage. This could be a real garage, a car boot, a college dorm, a sitting room couch, a bedroom, or somewhere else that is small and that you would not expect a business to start out, much less see success. It is basically going to be some kind of unconventional space for a business. Even some startups were able to establish themselves from a food café or something similar.

This is going to be a type of mental model is all about utilizing the free space that is available to start up your venture. First off, it can be cost-efficient because you do not have to worry about paying business rent to a startup. You just need to have a little space. This one is all about the sheer passion that comes from doing this whole process, rather than the sophisticated space from where you started the business. Some examples of people who fit into the Big Dreams Garage mental model will include:

Steve Jobs

At just 20 years old, Jobs was able to start up the company known as Apple with his friend Wozniak. This company was started in the basement of Job's parent's garage. To get the capital that was needed to start this venture, the $1350, Jobs sold off his Volkswagen microbus and then Wozniak sold his Hewlett-Packard calculator. During this time, Steve Jobs also dropped out of college to pursue the dream venture that was his at the time. And today, Apple is a company that is known all around the world.

Bill Gates

Staying along with the same idea with this one, we are going to move over to the start of Bill Gates and the Microsoft company. Bill Gates, with the help of his college friend Paul Allen, saw an advertisement in the magazine known as Popular Electronics. This advertising was looking for someone who could work with the Altair 8800 programming language.

Bill Gates and Paul Allen saw this as a really big opportunity for them to get ahead, and they decided to go straight for it. At this time, Gates dropped out of

Harvard University to pursue his dream venture. It was a matter of the urgency of now. This shows us that if something is not that urgent, and it is not so pressing to you, then it is time to just kick it out and not pay any attention to it any longer.

Richard Branson

The next person that we are going to take a look at with this kind of mental model is going to be Richard Branson. Branson started from the streets, as a kid hawker who sold Christmas trees. Eventually, though, he rose up and established a magazine business from the Churchyard. Branson is the most famous for his enterprise brand, known as Virgin Group. Under this enterprise, there are a few different options including:

1. Virgin Atlantic: This is an airline company
2. Virgin Galactica: This is a space technology company
3. Virgin Records: This is a well-known record production company.

Just like what we saw with Elon Musk, Branson's Virgin Group was able to break out of its core and cut across a lot of diverse fields in the process. At this point, Branson owns almost 400 companies under this umbrella group, and not all of them are going to be in the same field either.

Chapter 11: A Mastermind Alliance

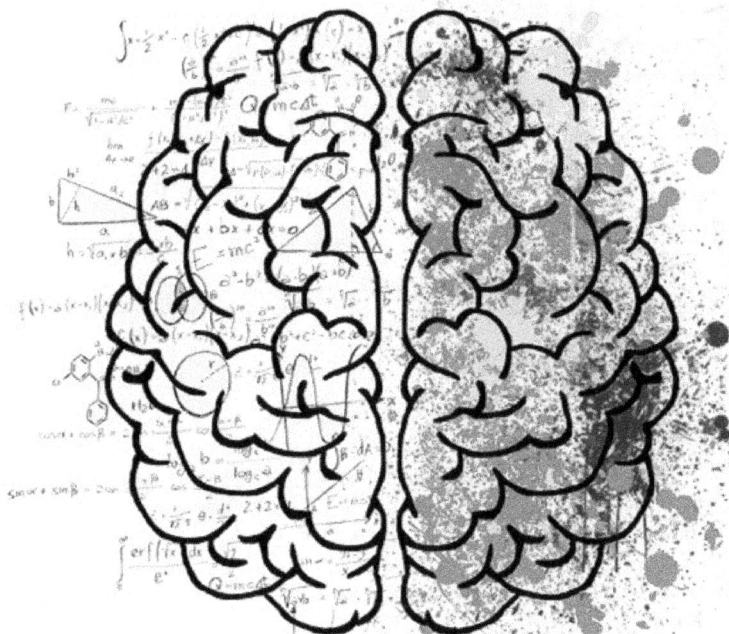

The next topic that we need to take a look at is going to be the mastermind alliance. This is going to be based on the master-master relationship. This is a type of alliance between independent, yet mutually interdependent persons with the aim of them all pulling together and consolidating their respective mental resources so that they are all able to meet their own goals.

The world is going to have a lot of examples out there of the master to servant relationships. This is often going to result in subjugation and domination, along with some level of exploitation of the vulnerable party in that relationship. Those who have instead chosen to go with the mastermind alliance are going to be rare and few overall. Probably, this deliberate scarcity of the mastermind alliances is out of the desire of most humans to either rule or be the one who is ruled over in the relationship.

While it is possible to have these mastermind alliances in a lot of different spheres, including in technology, science, education, religion, and politics, one of the most unique mastermind alliances that we are able to take a look at are going to show up in the sphere of entrepreneurial startups that can cut across a lot of diverse fields.

Looking a bit closer at some entrepreneurial startups, some of the ones that are the most successful in the world right now are going to be the ones driven by a unique mastermind alliance, one that is made up of passion mates. Not passion in terms of them being in a romantic relationship, but the passion in terms of pursuing a certain adventure. We are going to take a look at some of the examples out there when it comes to these mastermind alliances that are created out of the passionate entrepreneurial adventures.

The Importance of Having This Passion Mate

If you are young and you already know of a close friend of yours who would share a passion for a specific skill, know that you have not just found yourself a soul mate, but also a mind mate, a master mate, and someone who can be your passion mate. Some examples of these that we have seen throughout time include:

1. Zuckerberg and Eduardo Saverin
2. Larry Page and Sergey Bring
3. Bill Gates and Paul Allen
4. Steve Jobs and Steve Wozniak
5. Warren Buffet and Charlie Munger

Nonetheless, remember that it is never too late in the process to learn how to catch up to all of this. The earlier is the better because the biggest problem with this is that when you start a family, get married, and more, then things change, priorities shift, and it is harder to get the results that you want.

Pursuing your passion can be lonely if you are trying to do it all on your own, and if you don't have someone close to you to share all of this with. Chinese proverbs often say that "if you want to walk fast, walk alone. But if you want to walk far, walk with others." A passion mate can help you to walk that far, and even further than you would imagine from before.

The Importance of Forming One of These Alliances

A mastermind alliance is not just going to be about sharing thoughts and other information for the startup. It is going to be a fusion of the minds. It is going to be a dissolution of your separate minds so it becomes one common mind. Very few startups that began with just one person running them were able to walk that far, even though they were able to start with a bit more speed than others.

Yes, there is a reason to have some of these sprints, but there is also a reason that there are marathons around. A sprinter is hardly going to fit into the marathon, and the marathoner is hardly going to be able to fit in with the sprinter because they are each created in a different manner. This means that in the beginning, you have to be able to ask yourself if you are a marathoner or a sprinter. The answer that you get to this question is going to help you know where to start.

The Mastermind Mental Model

Now that we have had some time to talk about what the mastermind alliance is all about, it is time to work with the mental model and see how this is all going to come together. Think of it this way, did it just occur to these groupings to come together and form a pair to start a business? Even friends can be mean with each other when it comes to core mind investments. While you would think that this process would make things a bit easier, there are some times when things don't go the way that we want, and in some cases, friends will keep close secrets from one another.

Even these people and group pairings that we have talked about in this guidebook didn't have just one friend to work with. They had several. So, why didn't each go alone? As we all know, and as we can see from the tone of this book, it all begins in the mind. To embrace one of these passion mates towards an endeavor that is skillful and successful is going to be a matter of having a unique mind craft.

Your goal here is to seek out a passionate peer who has a similar mind. You know, whether this is consciously or not, that you are not able to capture this heavily potential moment all on your own. And any further delay means that the heavy expectancy is going to be delivered beyond you, by someone else. So, if you come to the ultimate conclusion that you are going to need someone to lend you a helping hand along the way, you have to make sure that you don't end up missing out on this opportunity or feeling overwhelmed in the process.

Chapter 12: Shifting Your Paradigm to Work with Mental Models

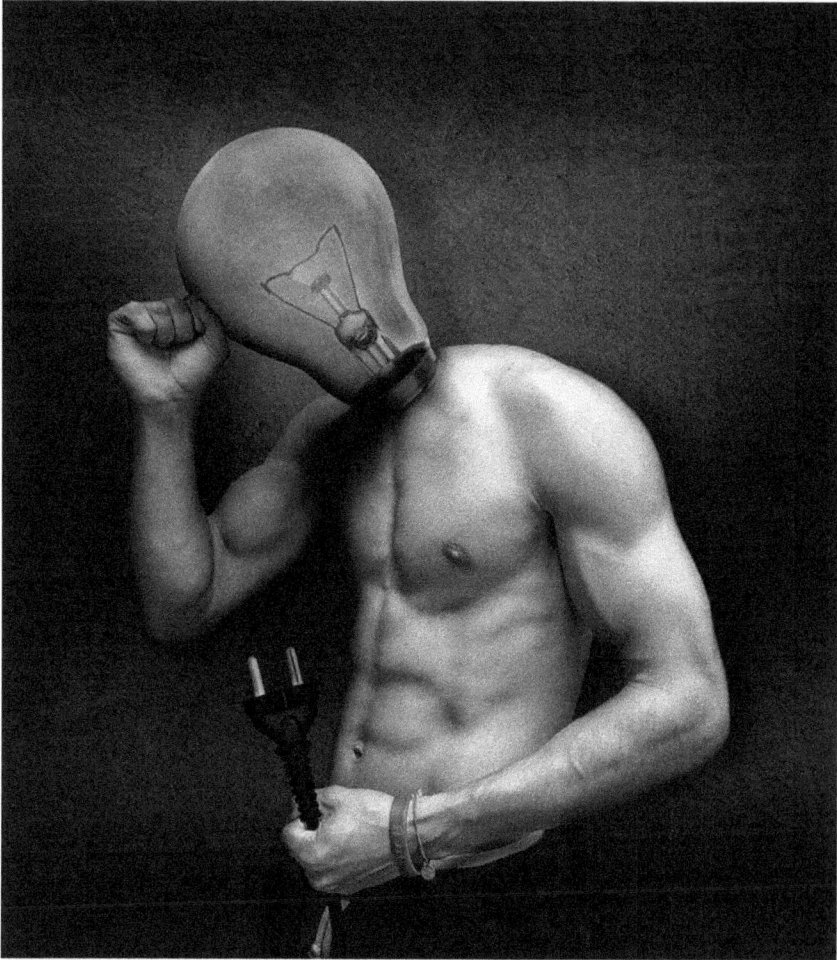

At this point, we have spent a good deal of time looking at these mental models and some of the great things that you are able to do with them. But it is important for you to work with these in order to improve your life and make sure that you are able to make good decisions and see some results in no time. But for some people, changing their old habits and moving over to using these mental models, and understanding how they work, can be a challenge.

In this chapter, we are going to explore the option of paradigm-shifting. This is going to be a radical and irreversible shifting to a new way of thinking and doing things. Why would we want to embrace this kind of shifting when it seems so strong and hard to do?

There are actually a few different reasons that can make it so important to embrace this kind of paradigm-shifting. One of the main reasons is that as great as any model really is, we have to remember that it is never going to be perfect. Because of this, a model is going to be just the best-fit depiction of reality. But the reality that we are in, and that we see, is never going to be perfect and it is always changing.

Reality, just like our clouds, is going to shift and change over time. Reality is in a constant state of motion, even though it is true that our focus is going to stagnate, and keep changing each and every moment. Hence, a model that was once a best-fit depiction of a specific reality will soon no longer be a best-fit when the reality ends up changing or ceases to be completely.

While a fixed mindset model is going to hold to a certain mental model as being the absolute (such as seeing it as the only good one, seeing it as the answer to everything, and turning to it in each scenario), a growth mindset is going to hold that a certain given model is going to be like a pair of oars that will enable it to navigate from one end of the shore over to the next.

With this analogy, we see that a fixed mindset is going to hold tightly onto the water as its end, and this could risk some drowning when we are swimming. But when we focus our attention on more of a growth mindset, we know that the water is a medium that can help us to travel from one end to the next.

Any time that you are working with these mental models, we have to remember that working with a fixed mindset is not always going to be a good thing. It is going to provide us with a really limited relevant range beyond which it becomes not just obsolete, but it could become a burden that is dangerous to stick with. Changing over to some growth mindsets could be the answer that you need to open up to these mental models, and actually get them to work for you.

A fixed mindset is going to limit us. It is going to see that a mental model is going to be the one and ultimate solution, or an end in itself. On the other hand, a growth mindset is going to see that these mental models are not absolute, but they can be a great tool to work on. This allows for the potential to craft up some new solutions along the way.

The fatality of having to look at these mental models just as a solution is that we end up clinging to the old tools that are no longer effective or efficient. Imagine that you stick to the tools that were used by the Homo Habilis in order to do food processing and farming. It is either that the evolution clock stops, or the species is going to become extinct, and we certainly don't want to see the latter as part of our destiny.

When we learn how to see some of these mental models as tools, we find that it is easier to understand that they are not just going to be a solution in themselves, but they become a means that we can use to reach our solution. Just as a pair of oars are not going to be our hands, and they are not our destiny, but they can be our means of reaching our destiny.

Believing is not always a bad thing. However, there are going to be certain beliefs that are more negative that end up being limiting or destructive to us. The most important thing to remember and understand here is the nature of the belief. A belief no matter if it is positive or negative is going to emanate from a lack of knowledge. It is more of a placeholder than anything else. As soon as you are able to find the right content to fill in this void, then it is unnecessary to have that placeholder any longer.

For example, at one point or another in history, some people thought that the world had to be flat. But, when the knowledge came out that the world is a sphere instead, the belief died its natural death. In the past, the idea that the earth was flat was a very simple placeholder for the lack of knowledge that people of that time had when it came to the true shape of the earth.

Thus, a belief is going to exist in the absence of knowledge. Where there is absolute knowledge, there will no longer be any beliefs in the process. A belief is just the natural mental way of the human mind to try and free up some of its energy from the anxiety that it gets from not knowing. Yet, a belief, if strongly held, is able to yield some complacency, and this is going to hinder some of the discovery and exploration that needs to happen.

In this regard, you need to make sure that you don't hold yourself a slave to beliefs. You need to be able to seek to understand their true nature and free yourself from their binding attachment. I believe not because I hold the belief to be true, but because I haven't found the truth yet.

Like beliefs that are no longer relevant when you receive some new knowledge, the old mental models that no longer fit into the modern world need to be left alone to die in the old ways.

We have to learn how to think of these mental models as a kind of tool that will help us to think better, and even to make some better decisions. But we have to understand that as tools, they can be changed, and they don't have to be used forever in the same manner. When we find better tools, or newer tools that work for us, it is not necessary to hold onto the tools that no longer serve the purpose that you need.

Letting go can be really hard for a lot of people. They like the mental model that they have. They may think that this mental model is the best one for them, and they won't need to change. And letting go of it is not going to work well for them. But being more flexible in the process, and learning when to use a tool, and when it is time to let it go, is going to make sure that you get the most out of these mental models.

Conclusion

Thank for making it through to the end of *Mental Models*, let's hope it was informative and able to provide you with all of the tools you need to achieve your goals whatever they may be.

The next step is to get started with using some of these mental models for our own needs. There are so many different types of mental models, and we tried to go through some of the most effective ones, the ones that will help you to make decisions, manage your time, and actually get things done. When you have the system in place that the mental model is able to provide to you, you will find that it is so much easier to get the results that you want. Your mind is now more free to think creatively, rather than focusing on things that are not all that important to you.

This guidebook took some time to look at the different mental models that are available to you. We discussed what these mental models are all about, some of the best mental models that can work for you, and the mental models and how they work with different situations in your life. This can help us to see all of the different things that come with them and will ensure that we are also using them in the right situations.

When you are ready to start freeing up your mind and seeing results with using these mental models for yourself, make sure to check out this guidebook to help you get started.

www.ingramcontent.com/pod-product-compliance
Lightning Source LLC
Chambersburg PA
CBHW050725030426
42336CB00012B/1421